ACQ-6748

W9-BCB-884

MAKING
YOUR
CLASSROOM
WORK

∨132

MAKING YOUR CLASSROOM WORK

Tried and True Organization and
Management Strategies

Carol Ross

Pembroke Publishers Limited

LIBRARY

To Jill. She made me do it! And I'm glad she did.

and

To Don, my husband, whose comment "YOU'RE going to write a book?" was just what I needed!

® 1994 Pembroke Publishers Limited
   538 Hood Road
   Markham, Ontario L3R 3K9

All rights reserved.

No part of this publication may be reproduced in any form or by any means, electronic or mechanical, including photocopy, recording, or any information or retrieval system, without permission in writing from the publisher.

Canadian Cataloguing in Publication Data

Ross, Carol (Carol A.)
   Making your classroom work

Includes index.
ISBN 1-55138-035-8

1. Classroom management.   2. Classroom environment.
I. Title.

LB3013.R67 1994   372.11'02   C94-931818-3

Editor: Margaret Hoogeveen
Design: John Zehethofer
Typesetting: Jay Tee Graphics Ltd.

This book was produced with the generous assistance of the government of Ontario through the Ministry of Culture, Tourism and Recreation.

Printed and bound in Canada by Webcom
9 8 7 6 5 4 3 2

Contents

Preface

Nobody warned me when I decided to become a teacher that there was more to this job than teaching. Over the past 20 years I have, not always willingly and sometimes unwittingly, served as a drill sergeant, confidante, record keeper, referee, fitness expert, comedian, guidance counsellor, timekeeper, computer consultant, friend, coach, environmental activist, interior designer, nutritionist, sex ed instructor, surrogate parent, actor or strategist, and entertainer. All this without even leaving the classroom!

We all need a little help in wearing our various hats and in handling the 101 challenges put before us every day in the classroom. Over the years, I've discovered that organization and management were the keys to sanity and success. This was, for some reason, a well-kept secret in university, where we were led to believe that if we mastered content and curriculum, we would somehow cope with the rest.

This how-to guide is written for both the seasoned and the novice teacher, for those who are struggling to keep chaos under control and those who simply wish to fine-tune their techniques. My tone may be slightly caustic — I'm a survivor, after all — but I'm a survivor who still finds the job of teaching to be a satisfying and creative career. Try some of the suggestions and strategies I've collected from my personal experience and from the experience of trusted colleagues. They're tried and true!

Acknowledgements

I would like to thank all the staff of Jasper Elementary School, whose collective expertise and ability to see the lighter side of teaching has kept me motivated and sane for the past 20 years.

1

Setting Up Your Classroom

or

Preparing for the Days of Necessity

The fable of the ant and the grasshopper contains what could well be the guiding principle for teachers: "It is best to prepare for the days of necessity." At no time is this more true than the beginning of the school year when the autumn preparations for teachers are as predictable as the signs of autumn in nature. Schools are abuzz with activity in those days prior to the arrival of students. These preparation days enable you to get your room organized as well as meet together as a staff. If it seems as though there are a million and one things to do, that's because there are!

Begin with the empty classroom. Keep in mind that acquiring all the furniture, equipment, and supplies for your classroom is but your first challenge. Your second will be to arrange everything. Try to take into account traffic flow patterns, accessibility, visibility, efficiency, and aesthetics. Although not everyone has an interior designer's eye for this aspect of room design, aim for practicality. Be prepared to arrange and then rearrange until you find a plan that suits your needs and those of your soon-to-be-arriving students.

Teacher's Desk

To begin with, make sure you have a comfortable chair. You may not spend much time in it when your students are there, but planning lessons and marking papers is a sit-down activity.

Now look over the desk. Is there a drawer with dividers in it for file folders? This will be a convenient place to keep files on individual students, as well as long-range plans, checklists, professional correspondence, and outlines of school procedures and policies. If you haven't got a drawer, use a milk crate or sturdy box and keep it near your desk.

A stacking tray on top of your desk is very functional. This will keep accessible any worksheets, notices, newsletters, and subject file folders currently in use.

Collect some essential items for storage in either a desk organizer or a second drawer:

- scissors (not small student scissors, but a pair of good-quality, sharp ones with your name engraved on them)
- a glue stick
- tape: masking tape, clear tape, and colored book-binding tape (expensive but invaluable for labelling binders, shelves, and containers)
- a stapler, staples, and a staple remover
- correction fluid
- highlighters
- pins (The ones with the colored plastic heads are easiest to use.)
- paper clips in a variety of sizes
- elastics in a variety of sizes and thicknesses
- a calculator
- sticky tack (This works much better than masking tape: it doesn't remove paint and it's reusable.)
- pens
- felt pens (Mr. Sketch last forever.)
- overhead pens
- a ruler
- pencils
- note cards (for thank-you and sunshine notes)
- sticky-back note pads

TRIED 'N TRUE

How to avoid "losing" your pencils
Instead of the standard yellow HB variety, buy yourself
a package of uniquely marked pencils. When they are
borrowed, as they surely will be, you will be able to
track them down.

Here are some not-so-essential items that can make life easier
for you:

- a timer (one that can be set for up to 20 minutes)
- breath mints (Coffee breath or garlic breath can be really offensive, as can heavy perfume or after-shave.)
- cough lozenges
- hand lotion
- a razor-sharp craft knife
- bandages
- a hammer and nails
- a screwdriver
- candles (for birthday celebrations and science demonstrations)
- pre-inked stamps
- stickers (a variety)
- a set of cards numbered to correspond with the number of students in your class (handy for a variety of things, including selection of groups) (See page 29.)
- a needle and thread
- matches (for science experiments and art). Hide these well.
- a glue gun (preferably the cold type)
- a whistle
- colored chalk
- a chalk holder

When deciding on the location of your desk, make sure you
will have clear visibility of all student desks as well as the door
to the classroom. Locate your desk near either built-in shelves
or a movable book shelf. A number of resources, such as curriculum guides, teacher's manuals, and professional resources,
can really clutter up a desk, yet you need to have them within
arm's reach.

Near Your Desk

You'll find it easiest if you keep your filing cabinet near your desk. Also, a bulletin board or blackboard nearby can be quite handy. On it you can pin little reminders to yourself or jot down students' names for one reason or another.

Find a place for the following items near your desk but not on it or in it:

- a three-hole punch (If you can, invest in the "Cadillac" variety, the type that can punch a whole class set at one time.)
- a small paper cutter with a protective catch
- a tray or box for usable scrap paper
- tissue
- a metre or yard stick
- a container for collecting small lost-and-found items
- extra chalk and brushes
- a number of plastic garbage bags
- an electric pencil sharpener (a bit noisy but a real timesaver)

Other Essential Classroom Equipment

If you can spare some time before classes begin, locate the following pieces of essential audiovisual equipment. Also, learn how to use them.

- an overhead projector (Be sure to find out where the spare bulbs are kept and learn how to insert one.)
- a tape-recorder (Try to get one with a microphone and earphones.)
- a record player
- a Polaroid camera with extra film
- a wall-mounted screen
- a movable trolley with shelves (This is ideal for holding an overhead projector and can also be used to transport materials when you're setting up a bulletin-board display.)
- a non-adjustable stool (The adjustable ones wiggle and squeak. Besides, someone always changes the adjustment on you.)
- additional tables (usually one or two is sufficient)
- extra chairs
- precut commercially made letters in a variety of sizes and colors
- plastic wash basins (Use these as assignment collection trays. Make sure they are large enough to hold notebooks and

workbooks. Label these clearly and store them on a shelf or table near your desk. Use these to carry your work home — briefcases were not designed with elementary teachers in mind!)
- Small blackboards for each student

TRIED 'N TRUE

Recycled individual blackboards

Mini-blackboards, approximately 12 inches by 20 inches (30 cm by 50 cm), can be cut from old blackboards that are being replaced. Get one for each student if you can. These are ideal for use in a variety of subjects. Students can hold them up to show you their work and you can see immediately who needs help. Each student can keep a piece of chalk in a sock stored in his or her desk. This will allow you to make use of the blackboards on the spur of the moment and for brief questions.

Bulletin Boards

Commercially produced or homemade borders on your bulletin boards really liven up a room and make your displays look professional.

For a first-rate job, make a professional-looking background using sticky-backed vinyl, which is fire-rated. As another option, use colored paper on rolls, which can be cut to measure and mounted. If staples are removed carefully, it will last for a year. Also, keep in mind that bulletin boards can be ordered in various colors and sizes. *If you should be so lucky!*

TRIED 'N TRUE

Precut letters

One of the best investments you can make is to purchase a set of commercially produced precut letters for use on your bulletin boards. These will last for years if you remove them carefully and store them in small boxes labelled by size and color. A great investment.

You will be much more organized if you assign a specific purpose to each of your bulletin boards. Reserve a small one near the door of your classroom to post a laminated month-long calendar. On this you can record important events, any special notices, the fire-drill procedure, the class list, the weekly timetable, a homework chart, and reminders to students regarding library books, art supplies, permission slips, or special phys ed requirements.

Assign some bulletin boards for particular subject areas. This will ensure that you always keep them current and use them as a teaching tool.

Create a few permanent displays. These can serve as visual cues or reminders to students. For example, you could display some of the following:

- the printed or cursive alphabet
- work/study habits
- place value charts
- student rights and responsibilities (see pages 47 and 49)
- number line
- the steps in solving a problem
- "Someone Special" (see page 7)

TRIED 'N TRUE

Hanging with sticky tack
If you are short on bulletin board space, permanent displays may be hung on blank walls using sticky tack, which will hold forever especially if used properly. Make small balls and attach to the back of your chart in several locations without pressing the balls flat. Once you have the chart in place on the wall, press down each ball separately. It really works!

Teacher supply stores and school supply catalogues carry a wide variety of commercially produced bulletin-board displays. Prices vary greatly so shop around. These can be great timesavers as long as you check on a few things first. They must use the proper units of measurement if they are math related. If you will be using them for a geography unit, make sure they are relevant to the states or provinces that you'll be covering. Ensure that the material reinforces concepts in accordance with your curriculum.

Of course, students' work should be displayed on some of your bulletin boards. To give their work a professional finish, it can be mounted on a piece of colored construction paper. Use pins instead of glue or tape. You can then save the mounting paper for future student displays. *REMEMBER: If you display student work, make sure you display samples by ALL your students.*

A bulletin board in the hallway outside your room is an excellent location for displays of student work. Be assured, it will be read or viewed by your colleagues, students from all grades, as well as parents. By letting your students know ahead of time that their work is going to be displayed, you will be giving them additional motivation to produce a piece of work of which they'll be proud.

For future reference, keep a record of your best bulletin-board ideas in a folder or recipe box. Use your Polaroid to snap a photo or quickly sketch the idea.

TRIED 'N TRUE

The "Someone Special" bulletin board

A "Someone Special/Personality of the Week" bulletin-board display works wonders for self-esteem. Each week, a different student is featured. Besides posting a chart that lists likes, dislikes, hobbies, and interests, the students can bring in photographs and other memorabilia. For the first week of school, highlight yourself to give the students an opportunity to learn about their teacher as a person.

In the upper elementary grades, bulletin-board monitors are invaluable. Selecting letters for titles, removing old displays, and arranging new displays are all tasks that become boring for you but are loads of fun for students.

Students' Desks

Do a little legwork to ensure that your students' furniture will be safe and in usable condition. First, check all chairs to make sure that all four legs are level and that the rubber casings (those thingamajigs on the ends of the legs) are in place. One wobbly chair can drive everyone nuts. Then, make sure that the chair backs are secure, without cracks or sharp edges, and that screws, if any, are tight. Check desks for any obscene graffiti or missing rubber casings. If the desks have removable baskets, ensure that they move easily in and out and are not cracked or broken.

Next, ensure that the chair heights match the desk heights. And check that you have the right size for your age-group. A 16-inch chair is designed for an average Grade 6 student, a 15-inch chair for an average Grade 5 student. All this may be in vain, of course — have you ever seen a standard issue Grade 6 student? I haven't! *NOTE: Office suppliers still talk in inches and feet — they're not metricated, even the ones in Canada.*

These are all tasks that the school custodians should have attended to. They too, however, are scrambling to accomplish 101 last-minute chores. If you ensure that all furniture is in good repair before your students arrive, you won't be faced with any minor but irritating problems when you have a room full of eager students and you can't find the custodians.

Always have at least one more desk and chair than you think you'll need, based on your class list. A late registration can be a headache if you have nowhere for the new addition to sit. It would be embarrassing for the student as well as disruptive to your first day's routine.

Some teachers prefer desks with chairs attached for the simple reason that students love to tilt back in unattached chairs. Needless to say, it can be annoying and dangerous if someone tips over in the middle of a lesson!

Find out from the custodial staff if students can tape things onto their desks or leave supplies on them overnight. *HINT: Establishing a good rapport with the custodians will make life easier. You're the one who teaches in the classroom, however, so don't allow cleaning procedures to dictate how you manage your class.*

Seating Arrangements

On the first day of classes, 20 to 30 (or perhaps even more) new faces will appear in your doorway, so it is essential to have some method prepared to assist you in learning their names as quickly as possible. Organized seating arrangements help. Here are a number of options that work effectively.

Assigned Seats

Begin with seats arranged in rows. Have your students sit in alphabetical order, which will make it easier for you to learn their names and eliminates the need for name tags.

On the first day, place standing name tags on the desks before the students arrive. For primary grades, put the name tags on strings so the students can wear their names around their necks. They can then find the matching name card on the desk you have chosen for them.

To add a bit of fun for the students, use the jigsaw method, which involves cutting out and laminating pictures of foods, animals, or toys on cardboard. Cut these in half to form two jigsaw pieces. Attach one half to each student's desk and distribute the second half to students as they come in.

If you want simplicity, make up a seating plan with the names already filled in and draw it on chart paper. Post this at the front of the room and let your students find their seats.

Student-Selected Seats

This method is only for the brave-at heart or the foolish, I'm not sure which. Prepare stand-up name cards for the students' desks. As your students arrive, simply hand out the cards and let the students choose their own seats. Alternatively, you can have the students choose their seats and prepare their own standing name cards.

The simplest method is to prepare a blank seating plan on chart paper and post it at the front of the room. As students arrive, they can select a seat and fill in their names in the appropriate place on the chart. *WORD OF WARNING: Usually when students self-select, they will sit with friends. You have the options of rearranging seating if you see that certain combinations don't work or changing things around later, either once or on a monthly rotation.*

Filing Cabinet

An organized filing cabinet will save you hours of frustration. At least one locking drawer on your desk or filing cabinet is essential to safeguard items such as student money, matches, your razor-sharp craft knife, student medication (only if such is to be taken during schooltime), and all confidential records including standardized test scores, counsellors' reports, or letters of a personal nature from parents.

Organizing things at the start can help you maintain order later on. For example, if you have a three- or four-drawer cabinet, label it by subject area. If you have access to colored file folders, designate specific colors for specific subjects. If you only have access to beige folders, then differentiate by using a specific-colored felt pen for specific subject areas or by using stick-on tags, which come in a variety of colors.

If you must make your own folders, use either manilla or colored construction paper. Fold the paper in half so the back half is higher for labelling purposes and color code the files using one of the methods mentioned above.

Within each drawer use dividers to group folders into subject areas; for example, divide the language arts drawer into grammar, creative writing, journal topics, spelling, handwriting, and novel-centre activities. If you can index your filing cabinet, you are truly on your way to becoming concrete sequential! However, don't take it to heart if you file by pile. It may look disorganized to others, but *you* know where things are — don't you?

Shelves

Keeping large textbooks in student desks is not conducive to keeping a tidy desk, and the weight can often cause problems with removable baskets. Instead, store these textbooks on shelves, labelling the shelves according to subject area to ensure that the books are returned to their proper location. Colored binding tape labelled with permanent felt pen sticks well to shelves. Dictionaries, thesauruses, atlases, manipulative materials, games, and art supplies should also have a designated, labelled storage location.

Textbooks

Before the students arrive, ensure that you have the correct number of textbooks and readers if there are enough available for a class set. If at all possible, find a few spares to keep on hand for the students who forget to bring theirs from home.

TRIED 'N TRUE

Numbering texts

Inside the front cover, in permanent felt pen, number every textbook. The number in the textbook should correspond to a number you assign each student when their names are arranged in alphabetical order. When the students have homework, they take home the corresponding text. In this way, you can keep track of the location and condition of the texts throughout the year.

Welcome Back Theme

A good way to focus young minds during the first week is a welcome back theme. Decorate your room according to the theme and try to integrate it into a variety of activities in the first few days. Name cards for students, bulletin boards, a selection of library books that relate to your theme, an art assignment, read-aloud stories, learning centres, and creative-thinking activities can all be tied in to your theme.

Art Supplies

It's the wise teacher who stocks up on a variety of art supplies. Paints, brushes, pastels, charcoal, construction paper, and crepe and tissue paper are all usually supplied by the school. A number of items can only come from home. Ask your students to bring them in.

Add or subtract from the list below, and send the list home either during the first week or at meet-the-teacher night. Set aside shelving in your room to store these items and you won't be caught short when you're ready to begin an art lesson. These materials are also very useful for project work in other subject areas. Here are some ideas to start with:

- newspaper
- ice-cream buckets
- magazines
- cardboard tubes
- plastic containers with lids
- corks
- wallpaper books
- styrofoam trays
- fabric scraps
- egg cartons

- wool
- styrofoam chips
- thread
- strawberry baskets

- spoons
- spools
- old greeting cards
- film cannisters

Australian Rounders
An Excellent Recess Activity

Australian Rounders, a team sport, is a combination of soccer and baseball. The game is easy to learn, has few rules, is popular with all ages, and requires little equipment.

Equipment

- one soccer ball
- 4 discarded rubber bicycle tires, which serve as first, second, and third base as well as the pitcher's box
- removable plastic base

Rules of Play

- There are two teams — one in field and one "at bat."
- Field positions are the same as in baseball.
- The pitcher rolls the soccer ball along the ground toward home plate, which can be designated by a removable plastic base.
- The "batter" kicks the ball and runs to first base.
- If the kicked ball is caught in the air (on the fly), the batter is out.
- Otherwise, the "batter" can continue running until the ball is returned to the pitcher, who must be standing in the pitcher's tire.
- If the runner is between bases when the pitcher gets the ball back AND is in the pitcher's tire, the runner is out.
- There may be up to five runners on one base at one time as long as each has one foot inside the base tire.
- Every "batter" on the team gets a turn and then the teams switch.
- The ONLY way to put a runner out is to get the ball to the pitcher while the runner is between bases.

Recess/Playground Equipment

Classes are usually designated a few pieces of equipment for the students to play with at recess — often a variety of balls and perhaps a skipping rope. These should all be labelled clearly with your grade and room number and stored in a box near the door. Monitors can be assigned to take out and bring back this equipment at recess.

If your school does not provide equipment for each room, you might consider asking students to bring a supply for the class. You could also purchase two or three balls yourself. Australian rounders is an excellent recess activity. It's an invention from "Down Under" that combines the best attributes of soccer and baseball. All you need is four old rubber bicycle tires and a soccer ball.

Don't Forget To

____ Introduce yourself to non-teaching staff.
____ Collect and read the handbook on school policies and rules.
____ Find out where art and science supplies are located.
____ Locate AV equipment and learn use and signout procedures.
____ Collect the recess/lunch supervision schedule.
____ Find a "mentor" among experienced staff members.
____ Collect a copy of fire-drill procedures.
____ Familiarize yourself with fire-drill procedures.
____ Find out pertinent information about the photocopier.
____ Collect any classroom supplies that are provided by the school.
____ Locate and read a copy of the current teaching contract.
____ Organize your desk and situate it in an advantageous spot.
____ Obtain necessary teacher supplies.
____ Familiarize yourself with the operation of classrom AV equipment.

_____ Prepare bulletin-board borders, backgrounds, and titles.

_____ Display the timetable, class list, special notices, and classroom calendar.

_____ Set up permanent displays such as "Somone Special" with information about you.

_____ Count and check over student desks.

_____ Arrange desks according to your "Year Beginning" plan.

_____ Make name tags.

_____ Label shelves.

_____ Collect and number texts and readers.

_____ Choose a "Welcome Back" theme and plan a number of activities based on your theme.

_____ Organize and label playground equipment for recess.

_____ Make a list of art supplies to be brought from home.

_____ Purchase and label a number of plastic wash basins.

_____ Label filing cabinet by subject area.

_____ Find small-tipped permanent felt pens for labelling supplies.

_____ Prepare a supply check list.

_____ Label your personal supplies.

_____ Prepare class lists and put them beside any containers where students need to check off their names.

_____ Label containers for student scissors and glue.

_____ Prepare a set of cards with numbers corresponding to the number of students.

_____ Prepare attendance cards and a pocket chart.

_____ Prepare a "Washroom Visit" chart.

_____ Photocopy the list of "33 Ways to Dismiss" and post it on your personal bulletin board.

_____ Prepare a "Classroom Monitors" bulletin board.

_____ Prepare your "Fine System" chart.

_____ Set up a classroom mailbox for absent students' work.

_____ Prepare an overhead of the UN Declaration of the Rights of the Child.

_____ Prepare your "Classroom Goals" blank chart.

_____ Prepare and laminate a large class timetable.

2

Classroom Routines

or

Starting Off on the Right Foot

As goes the first day, so goes the week.
As goes the first week, so goes the year.
— anonymous

Physically organizing your classroom is but the first step. The second and perhaps more challenging step is to establish classroom routines. These will enable you to establish a classroom climate conducive to learning and productive thinking. Above and beyond this primary objective, you'll get some other benefits. Clearly defined routines, procedures, rights, and responsibilities allow your students to know what is expected of them. By setting up goals for both individuals and the class as a whole, you will enable all class members to work to their potential. Also, your management strategies will create an environment that will nurture and develop each student's self-esteem.

Be sure to give classroom organization and routines careful consideration *before* your students arrive on that first day. Taking the time to identify and clarify these details and communicate them clearly to your students will be worth it. The effort expended will pay back tenfold later in the year. If you wait until a situation arises that you haven't thought through (perhaps forgotten homework, dismissal time, or late students) and you haven't clearly established a routine, you risk being labelled unfair or inconsistent.

Keep in mind that your style of classroom management can be as personal as your handwriting. What works for one person may not be successful for another. THE KEY IS CONSISTENCY! Your approach to routines, expectations, and consequences will make all the difference in establishing and maintaining a healthy and productive classroom climate. *NOTE: Some routines may be dictated by school policy. Make sure that you familiarize yourself with this document and consult with a mentor or colleague if you have any doubts.*

Care of Students' Personal Supplies

Nothing is more annoying than being interrupted in a lesson by the refrain, "Teacher, someone stole my ..." By giving your students the opportunity to label everything in advance, you give them the message that it is not your responsibility to look after their supplies. Tracking down misplaced supplies will also be much easier.

Labelling. Prevent the problems before they happen. Small-tipped permanent felt pens and book-binding tape are recommended for labelling any supplies that belong to students. Everything from scissors, glue, felt pens, pencils, erasers, and binders to phys ed clothes and shoes can be marked with either student initials or their own secret symbol.

Checking supplies. As a monthly routine, do a supply check. It only takes ten minutes and it reminds your students to keep their supplies up to date. Give them until the end of the week after your supply check to round up the missing supplies. Often it is only a case of students bringing back to school those supplies they had taken home to work on a project.

The supply check doubles as an opportunity to have students clean out their desks thoroughly. It is amazing what can be found jammed in a messy desk: lost permission forms, house keys, retainers, money, lumps of your sticky tack, half-eaten recess snacks. The list is endless! Ask the students to place their supplies out on top of their desks. You can circulate with your checklist or assign a student this task. Alternatively you can ask your students to hold up each supply as you call it out. If any supplies are missing, the students can record it in their homework book as a reminder.

School supplies. If certain supplies are provided by the school, such as pencils, glue, or scissors, they should be labelled with your room and grade. You'll need to develop a system for any consumable items to ensure that students use them responsibly and are not wasteful.

For example, you could keep a container of a consumable item, such as pencils, on a table near your desk. Tape a class list on the container. When students take one, they put a check mark by their name. It becomes easy to identify anyone who is hoarding pencils or just being careless about looking after them.

With young students, label items such as glue and scissors and then keep them in a box. When needed, these items can be distributed. No more students cutting their hair when bored! No more leaky glue in a desk or, worse yet, students eating glue!

TRIED 'N TRUE

A no-fail exchange system

If students are responsible for providing their own supplies but have temporarily run out of an item and need to borrow from you, use an exchange system: in order to borrow an item such as a pencil or ruler, students must give you something else, a shoe, for example. They get the shoe back only when they return the borrowed item. You can be sure they won't be going far!

Taking Attendance

One of the many tasks described collectively as "administrivia," taking attendance must be done consistently or you will incur the wrath of the school secretary. Before you resort to tearing your hair out because "these columns in my register just don't add up!" try some of these tactics for simplifying or adding variety to this sometimes tedious chore.

Pocket chart. Make up or purchase a pocket chart with a transparent front. Hung on the wall, this chart can display name cards for a whole class. As students arrive, they can slip out their name cards, flip them over, and slip them back in, indicating their presence. Each name card has the same name on both sides but in two distinct colors, one for morning attendance and one for afternoon attendance. A quick glance at the chart tells you who is absent.

Question and answer. If you prefer calling attendance, give the students a question they must answer when their name is called. For example, they could name fruits, vegetables, animals, words beginning with a particular letter, a basic fact or times table, and so on.

Delegating. Ask your "Someone Special/Personality of the Week" to call attendance and record the names of absent students. Be sure to check the accuracy of his or her work.

NOTE: Depending on school procedures, attendance slips are either delivered to the office or picked up from each class. Accurate attendance taking is essential, especially if your school has a "Safe Arrival" program, whereby parents are phoned if their child is absent.

Dealing With Lates

You will find it least disruptive to your class and least embarrassing to the student if you establish a procedure that students will know to follow if they arrive late. They can either check in at the office immediately or enter the class and take their seat as quickly and quietly as possible. It will be up to you to follow up with the individual at a convenient time to determine the reason for lateness and to notify the office of his or her arrival, if not already done. Many schools will have a policy in place regarding students who are late. Always check first before establishing any procedures within the classroom.

If a student is rarely late, it is not something to worry about. If a student is arriving late on a regular basis, however, you should investigate. Begin by ascertaining the reason for the behavior. If the child simply dawdles on the way to school, a request to the parents to send him or her out the door five to ten minutes earlier may be all that is needed. If the child either sleeps in or has to get himself or herself ready for school in the morning because the parents have already left for work or are still asleep owing to shift work, the situation may be more difficult to resolve. Once again, communication with parents is essential and a team problem-solving approach rather than placing blame will result in more cooperation from the home. It may be necessary to initiate some form of incentive program to motivate the student. If you don't want to hear, "Honest! A burglar stole my alarm clock," then you'll have to give them a reason to be on time!

Washroom Visits

The essential bodily functions, which we don't think twice about at home, can become a teacher's nightmare. An "accident" will often happen if you don't allow a student to visit the washroom because he or she has already gone four times that day. The other scenario we all dread is the poor student frantically waving his or her hand to get permission to leave the room, but because you are attending to another situation in the room, you fail to notice. Aside from creating an embarrassing situation for the student, you will probably "hear from" the parents very shortly afterward. The moral of this story is, once again, have a routine or procedure in place that addresses these possibilities and make sure all students know it well.

Under normal circumstances, it is not unrealistic to expect students to ask permission to use the washroom. Let the children know, however, that if they are desperate, they can just go.

One situation to avoid is when more than one student of the same gender requests to leave the room at the same time. More often than not, some surreptitious motive lurks in their minds. In order to monitor this behavior, make a simple chart to hang on the bulletin board by the door. When a student leaves the room, have him or her flip over the card that says "Occupied" or "Busy" under the appropriate label ("Boys" or "Girls"). Upon his or her return, the card should be flipped again so that it now says "Unoccupied," "Empty," or some such phrase. In this way you can tell at a glance if the washroom is free.

Discuss with the students what constitutes a reasonable length of time to be gone from the room. Emphasize that a visit to the washroom should not be seen as an opportunity to examine all the bulletin boards in the hallway, count floor tiles, or observe other classes in progress. *A WORD OF WARNING: Ensure that students don't take a pencil or pen with them when they go to the washroom. Graffiti on washroom walls can be a real problem!*

Drinks From the Water Fountain

According to a Grade 1 student who is an expert on the subject of water fountains, "Math makes you real thirsty!" If you're lucky enough to have a fountain in your room, quenching of tiny thirsts becomes less of a problem. In this case, getting a drink should not be something for which a student requires permission. After all, you have more pressing matters to attend to in the course of a day. Emphasize though, that having the freedom to get a drink when they want it, is a privilege, something that should not be abused.

There are certain times when the water fountain should be out of bounds, even if it's in the classroom. These include times when the teacher, any student, or a guest is talking to the whole class or during a test.

If the water fountain is in the classroom, always follow two simple rules: no more than one person at the fountain at one time and no visiting with friends along the way. When students come in from recess or lunch break, the fountain may be in demand. To alleviate this problem, limit them to three seconds (3000, 2000, 1000) per student and, if they still can't line up in an orderly fashion, simply ask them all to sit down. That should get the message across!

If your room is not equipped with a fountain, avoid taking the whole class out to the fountain at one time, as you will inevitably end up with pushing and talking, which will be both disruptive to other classes and a big waste of everyone's time. Instead, schedule fountain breaks into the morning and afternoon routine by sending the students out of the room in pairs at a specified time. Set a reasonable time limit for the fountain visit.

Unscheduled Interruptions

Unplanned visits by colleagues, parents, or students from other classrooms, minor emergencies, such as putting a bandage on a cut finger or locating an unplanned-for but essential piece of equipment in the classroom, will provide the perfect opportunity for students to "cut up" unless you clarify your expectations of their behavior in these situations. Probably the easiest solution is to have the students take a book out of their desks and read quietly. There should be no reason for them to get out of their desks at this time or visit with their neighbors. Make a point of reinforcing the behavior of those students who are being responsible and thank them for their cooperation.

Students love to hear what a good class they are, so if you are in the situation where you must disturb another teacher during class time, apologize to the students for interrupting them and thank them afterward for being so well mannered.

Teacher Leaving Room

Leaving your room unsupervised is not a wise move and should be avoided unless absolutely necessary. It only takes one student to get others going, and if, in the course of their misbehavior, someone gets injured you are responsible. In the rare instance where it is essential, ask your students to cooperate by remaining in their desks while you are out of the room and make your absence as short as humanly possible.

That First Five Minutes of the Day

Train yourself to be at the door of your classroom to greet the students when they arrive. The settling influence and welcoming atmosphere you create will be worth the extra little bit of effort. A few "spontaneous" personal comments to individuals as they pass through the door can really make a difference as to how students start the day: "Did you have a good sleep?" "That looks like a new haircut" "You look particularly keen today!" or "I like those colorful mitts."

Having a first assignment written on the board, such as a topic for a journal entry, a short handwriting lesson, or a message from you written in code, will give the students something to do while you check attendance. It will also serve as a meaningful way to "soak up" those few moments of transition time.

If there is homework to be handed in or permission forms to be collected, use a labelled plastic tub or basket. If you let your students know what you expect, they'll soon be putting their assignments in the appropriate location when they arrive. Beside the homework box, place a checklist on a clipboard with student names and dates. Students can check their names off when they hand in their work. You can then see at a glance whose homework is missing and you also have a record at the end of each month to put in your file for reporting purposes. More immediately, you avoid the situation of six or seven students surrounding you and badgering you with the inevitable refrains: "Where do you want my homework?" "What do I do with this form?" and "Can I give this to you now?" We must do all we can to make those first few minutes less stressful!

At the beginning of each month, establish a "Classroom Focus" as part of your routine. If your focus for that time period is printing and handwriting, begin each morning by having a small printing or handwriting lesson on the board. This becomes the first task of the day. You can try any number of monthly topics:

- RINGO (Reading Is Now Going On)
- Response Journals
- Creative Thinking
- Logical Thinking
- Personal Spelling Lists
- Paired Reading

By "blitzing" a topic for a month, a mini-routine is developed for that block of time and that particular focus.

The Last Ten Minutes of the Day

End-of-day routines are very important because that's when your students are most worn out and anxious to be gone, and your patience is waning rapidly! Homework must be organized and assigned if not done so earlier in the day. Reminders for the following day as well as newsletters, permission forms, and book orders will have to be passed out. Monitors may have jobs to do that will necessitate a number of students being out of their desks. All in all, it makes for a frantic finish if it gets out of hand. Before you cry out, "_____, give me strength," try the following strategy.

To begin, if students have a homework book, they should have it on their desks open to the day's date. Displayed on chart paper should be the following questions:

a) What homework do you have? Record this in your homework book.
b) What materials do you need? Gather any texts or supplies you need.
c) What do you need to bring from home tomorrow? Record this in your homework book.

d) Is your desk and the space around it tidy? If not, clean up.

At the beginning of the year, go through these questions together at the end of each day. Once students have mastered the routine, they can just read through the list silently and monitor themselves.

Spend a couple of minutes having the students verbally summarize the events of the day. This will refresh everyone's memory, and, just maybe, when your students go home and their parents ask them what they did in school today, their response will be something other than "nothing."

Thirty-Three Ways To Dismiss a Class

Dismiss 25 students at one time for recess, for lunch, for a specialist class, or at the end of the day and watch what happens! Chaos in the cloakroom, crowding and pushing at the doorway, an elbow in someone's eye, and running in the hallway. All of these behaviors that lead to conflict between students and discipline problems for you at dismissal time can easily be avoided. Send them off according to creative criteria. Try these, for starters:

1. month in which they were born
2. beginning letter of middle name
3. number of vowels in first name
4. first letter in middle name
5. number of syllables in last name
6. color of pants or skirt or dress
7. color of top or dress
8. color of hair
9. color of eyes
10. color of bed covering
11. color of the family dishes
12. color of bedroom walls
13. color of coat or jacket at school
14. color of house or apartment building
15. type of ties on shoes (velcro, laces, none)
16. type of top (short-sleeved, collar type, button up)
17. length of hair
18. beginning letter of mother's name
19. beginning letter of father's name

20. what they ate for breakfast
21. what they will have for lunch
22. number of children in family
23. number of older sisters
24. number of younger sisters
25. number of older brothers
26. number of younger brothers
27. phone number numerals
28. address numerals
29. type of pet
30. number of pets
31. number of times student has moved
32. places they have visited
33. movies they have seen

Keep this list handy and add categories as you think of them. It goes without saying that you must be sensitive to individual situations so that you don't embarrass anyone unintentionally. Students will catch out their classmates if they are leaving for a criteria that doesn't apply to them. Allow a few seconds between each category to give students time to clear out of the cloakroom and entry way.

TRIED 'N TRUE

A peaceful goodbye
Use of sign-language symbols with groups seated together is a very effective way of dismissing students because it requires them to focus their attention on the teacher. Assign each group a symbol for either different colors, autumn objects, animals, or Halloween words. Help them learn to recognize their symbols. When you're ready to dismiss them, you merely need to "sign" a group's symbol. These symbols can be used in other ways throughout the day for tasks such as collecting or handing up materials.

Dismissal, of course, can be streamlined. Simply dismiss on an individual basis as you see students indicating their readiness by either standing by their desks or sitting quietly. If it's the end of the day, say goodbye to your students at the door, asking the forgetful to show you that they have their homework and texts. Perhaps you can ask them a question along one of the following lines before you let them out the door:

1. a basic fact
2. a times-table fact
3. something you learned in science
4. name of capital city of _____
5. spelling of a particular word
6. an analogy, e.g., Labrador is to dog as parakeet is to _____
7. favorite singing group
8. something interesting that happened today
9. what you want to be when you grow up
10. where you'd like to go for a vacation

If students make mistakes on a question of fact, simply tell them the correct answer and have them repeat the question with its answer. You don't want to embarrass them or hold up the rest of the students. If the "hordes" start getting restless, ask every fourth or fifth student a question. They won't be keeping track to see who gets asked!

This is also an opportunity for you to comment briefly to individuals on something positive they did that day, or to make reference to an activity they're involved in after school. This really is a nice way to finish the day for both you and your students. For some, the positive comments they receive at school may be the only ones they hear all day.

Classroom Monitors

Most students love to help the teacher and will eagerly and willingly volunteer for almost any task. Giving the students input into the type of jobs, how they are selected, and the length of assignment to a job will give the students a feeling of participation in the management of the classroom.

A permanent bulletin-board display with students' names on cards makes it easy to reassign jobs on a weekly, biweekly, or monthly basis. Rotating students through every job or drawing names from a hat are two options available for selecting students.

Here are some suggestions for jobs that can be assigned to classroom monitors:

1. The **book monitor** distributes and collects texts, readers, notebooks, and binders.
2. The **paper monitor** distributes and collects worksheets and written assignments.
3. The **attendance monitor** takes attendance slips to the office.
4. The **errand monitor** goes on errands to the library, the office, and other classrooms.
5. The **blackboard monitor** cleans the boards and brushes.
6. The **cloakroom monitor** checks the cloakroom daily for items left on the floor, smelly lunches, and so on.
7. The **calendar monitor** records important upcoming events on a large write-on/wipe-off monthly calendar.
8. The **homework monitor** records assignments on the homework chart.
9. The **media monitor** sets up and puts away the overhead projector, pulls down the screen, and assists with the operation of the 16-mm projector and the tape-recorder.
10. The **lights monitor** turns off the lights when students leave the room.
11. The **recycling monitor** takes sorted paper, cans, or bottles to the school's central depot. If your school doesn't have a recycling program for paper, start one!

Another option would be to use your "Personality of the Week" to assist you with all jobs in the classroom during his or her special time.

Collecting Assignments

Whether it's worksheets, written assignments, notebooks, workbooks, or tests, a system is needed for collecting work if you want to be able to find your desk at the end of the day.

Using assigned monitors makes sense if an assignment is to be handed up at a specific time. If you want students to pass in work when they complete it, the use of labelled baskets or plastic bins is more practical. Keep a class checklist beside the bin and coach your students to check off their names as they hand something in.

When students are midway through an assignment, put the names of four to five randomly selected students on the board and direct them to bring their work to you when completed for immediate marking and feedback. This "spot-checking" will give you a feel for how well students understand your directions and will keep your students on their toes. You can also find out if they understand the concept you taught. You may, of course, provide comments on quality, neatness, and proofreading of work, but it's fine to save detailed comments for the final version.

No-Name Assignments

How many times have you shaken your head and asked yourself, "Whose paper is this, anyway?" It becomes quite easy, after a month or so, to recognize a student's printing or handwriting, but it can be time-consuming and a bit annoying if you have three or four papers with no names.

To encourage your students to remember to write their names, simply ask your paper monitor to check for names as he or she picks up the assignments. If your students are passing up their work, first ask them to have a neighbor check their names. If

TRIED 'N TRUE

No more no-name assignments

To avoid the problem of no-name assignments, impose a fine system. First, post a class list near your desk. Each time an assignment is handed in with no name, write a cent symbol in the space where their name should be on the assignment. Record the fine using a tally system beside his or her name on the checklist. For example,

Robin 𝖭𝖷𝖪 /

Students are responsible for bringing in their fine money and depositing it in a clear money jar kept on your desk. If they bring in five cents, they cross off the five tallies beside their name with a colored felt pen.

At a class meeting at the beginning of the year, the students determine how this money will be used. Encourage the students to contribute this money to a worthy cause at the end of the year.

Students are usually very conscientious about paying their fines and will often bring extra pennies and put them in the money jar as a charitable gesture. Parents have never complained about this system and it can be used just as well to deal with cloakroom "remains."

you're using the basket and checklist system, have a sign on the basket reminding them to put their names on their work.

Absent Students and Missed Work

With the myriad of activities that take place in any given class-room on any given day, it is sometimes amazing that you even realize that someone is absent, let alone that you remember to set aside any assignments that will have to be done. Therefore, you need to develop a routine for recording missed work and saving any worksheets, notices, or reminders that the returning student should have. As well, the length of a student's absence, the type of work missed, the ability of the student as well as his or her age are all factors to be considered when developing a plan for dealing with this situation. You might consider the following strategies.

A classroom mailbox. By stacking up, joining together, and labelling a class set of milk cartons, you can make a class mailbox. Alternatively, you can make up a class set of labelled file folders stored in a box. When monitors distribute worksheets or other handouts, they must ensure that these are put in any missing person's slot in the mailbox.

The buddy system. Assign every student a buddy. When students are away from school, their buddies must collect any assignments for their partners and then, when they return, explain the missed work and answer any questions they may have regarding what went on in their absence.

Individual meetings. By meeting with returned students, no matter what system you use to get them their assignments, you can check that they understand the nature of the assignments as well as reconfirm what their responsibilities are.

Grouping and Partnering Students

Everyone's worst memory of school usually relates to situations that involved being left out or last chosen. It's crushing to an individual's self-esteem as well as stressful for the classmate being forced to make a choice. A variety of methods for pairing or grouping are essential for a teacher's repertoire. For example, you could pull names or numbers from a hat, hand out cards from a playing deck (and match numbers), or even select by alphabetical order.

TRIED 'N TRUE

Numbered cards

If random pairing or grouping is required, use those cards you made numbered from "1" to the number of students in your class. Fan these cards like a deck in your hands and ask a student to select the number needed to form a group. Call out the numbers drawn and those students whose names correspond will form the first group or pair. It's a quick and fair system!

For some projects, you will want to choose the group composition quite carefully. For either heterogeneous or homogeneous groups, form the groups ahead of time. Tell the students you are doing this *before* saying, "You will be working in groups." Once those words have been uttered without the qualifier that you have set the groups yourself, students "tune out" of any further explanation you give about the assignment and begin the complicated but not so subtle process of getting their friends' attention. Nodding, making eye contact, whispering, squirming with excitement, and even dashing over to their imagined partner's desks are all behaviors you can expect. Meanwhile, those who know they won't be selected, slump in their chairs and visibly wilt at yet another opportunity for their egos to be deflated.

Getting Students' Attention

"Class!... Class!... Claaaaassssssss!" Sound familiar? Getting the attention of the whole class at one time and then holding your students' attention long enough to give instructions, set new tasks, or remind them of their responsibilities regarding behavior remains a skill that often separates the novice from the experienced teacher, the weak from the strong!

Here are a few tried and true methods gleaned from trial and error or observation of those often described as "master teachers":

• Have a stool at the front of the room. When you want their attention, sit on the stool and WAIT.

- Raise your hand above your head, stand still keeping your hand above your head, and WAIT.
- Use a signal phrase such as "Eyes on me" or "Ready." Say it only once, in a strong voice, and WAIT.
- With younger students, use the phrase "Gimme five." The five elements of this cue are 1) eyes on me, 2) mouth closed, 3) body turned to face teacher, 4) hands on desk, and 5) listening with both ears.

Praise is a remarkable tool. Catch the students behaving properly and reinforce their behavior with statements such as "I see Cindy's ready" and "Thanks, Pierre, for having your books out,"

If two or three students are very slow in responding, use proximity as an additional cue. Move over to where they are talking or fidgeting and make eye contact or physical contact by touching their desks. It's incredible what your presence can do. Never underestimate the power of fixing THE EYE on wayward students or setting THE EXPRESSION on your face. It really works!

Waiting is the hardest aspect of getting students' attention. If you proceed before everyone is listening, you are doomed to repeat yourself. The talkers will not be the only ones to miss out. Their neighbors will have more difficulty focusing on you.

Explain to the students what your expectations are with regard to listening. Establish your signal, practise it with your students frequently at the beginning of the year, and review the components of good listening until they are able to demonstrate them consistently. Time spent initially on this aspect of classroom management will be more than made up!

Varying the Ways Students May Respond

Asking all your students to sit quietly while you ask them questions one at a time is a sure-fire way to tune them out. Try to incorporate techniques that get all your students participating. You can have the whole class respond to a question in a variety of ways. Try these strategies for making things more interesting.

Blackboards. If you have access to individual blackboards, use them. The students can write their answers on these boards, and then hold them up facing you when you ask for the answer. This way you get immediate feedback from the entire class. If you position yourself near a student who is having difficulty, you can provide assistance while everybody is writing.

Labelled cards. Provide students with laminated Bristol board cards 2 inches by 8 inches (5 cm x 20 cm). Ask your students to label them at the long ends on both sides with the math operations signs (+, -, x, and /). Use them to have students show what kind of word problem you have read to them. For example,

> Marcos has seven candies. He gives his friend three. How many does he have left?
> (Student holds up card with the minus sign facing the teacher.)

You can also use cards like this for grammar activities, such as analyzing kinds of sentences by labelling them with a question mark, exclamation point, period, or IS (incomplete sentence).

Signing. You can implement an easy sign system for quick reviews and opinion surveys. Thumbs up means "yes," thumbs down means "no," and thumbs sideways means "I don't know."

Telling one another. "Turn and Tell Your Neighbour," is a handy way to ensure active participation, especially when the topic is one in which everyone is eager to share his or her thoughts. To make it more challenging, have your students then turn and tell another neighbour what the first person said to them. This forces them to be good listeners too!

Group response. If you can handle some noise, try a group response. "On the count of three, tell me." Students who are unsure of their answer can check their response against what they've heard.

Giving Clear Directions

During a typical school day, you may find yourself giving directions for everything from completing a questionnaire to using a tape-recorder, mixing paint to writing a friendly letter, planning a presentation to folding origami birds.

Under usual circumstances, whatever the task for which you need to provide instructions, you can be quite sure that many of your students won't get the message. A portion of students will not listen carefully, another group of students will listen to only the first few words of your explanation, and yet another group will appear to listen carefully and still not have a clue what you want them to do. You need to take some steps to reduce the number of casualties.

Always use your established teacher signal and *wait* until you have everyone's attention. Then state what you are going to give directions for. If the directions relate to a procedural matter with which the students are unfamiliar, state the directions concisely and then ask for volunteers to restate them. Finally have them turn and tell a neighbour and correct any mistakes for each other. Ask a volunteer to demonstrate, when appropriate.

If your directions relate to a procedural matter with which the students should be familiar, test their memory by asking them to tell you how something is to be done. Point out any errors immediately and restate correctly. Once again, you may also ask a volunteer to demonstrate, if appropriate.

If the directions relate to the completion of an assignment over several periods, list the directions in brief point form on chart paper so students have something to refer to every time they work on the assignment.

Once you have given the direction, and the students have either reviewed or repeated them, avoid repeating them for individuals. If the students know that they can get individual attention and explanations, they will not bother to listen to the group explanation. In situations like this, avoid giving them a lecture about how they should have been listening. Instead, ask them how they are going to deal with their problem. You can teach problem-solving strategies for such situations. For example, the students may politely and quietly ask a neighbor. They can observe what other students are doing and infer what they should be doing. Or they can simply think back to what they were doing during the directions, to see if that triggers their memory.

Some students will ask you to repeat directions, not because they weren't listening but because they lack self-confidence and are afraid to make a mistake. You will learn to know which students fall into this group. By asking them to tell you or a friend what they think you said and then reinforcing their correct response, they will see that they did, in fact, know what to do.

If more than a few students seem confused about the instructions, get the students' attention and review the directions once again. This is an indication that perhaps you were vague or used vocabulary that wasn't appropriate for the age of the students. Nobody's perfect! Always avoid imprecise, vague language and uncertain quantities. Words such as *many, several, few, sort of, big, small,* and *probably* do not provide any limitations or guidelines and can be easily misinterpreted.

Be aware that if you begin a set of instructions only to be interrupted to answer the door or speak to an unruly student, you should start over or at least have a volunteer repeat the directions given so far.

You will eventually give The Lecture to a student asking you to repeat your directions, only to find out that this was the student who was out of the room at the time, running an errand for you. Don't feel too bad — it happens to the best of us!

Transition Time

Changing from mathematics to language arts, switching from a teacher-directed lesson to learning centres, moving from the classroom to the gym and back, or waiting for the arrival of a guest speaker who is five minutes late are all examples of transition time. In terms of actual minutes in a day, these periods seem insignificant. It is during these changeovers, however, when the "crowd" becomes restless.

For starters, many minor discipline problems may arise, general noise levels increase, and spontaneous socializing takes place. Of course, no one expects a group of students to sit quietly all day long and ignore their classmates, but if peripheral distractions end up taking over each transition time, they will seriously cut into your day.

Smooth transitions are every teacher's goal, and, like every aspect of classroom routine, you will have to explain, practise, model, and reinforce.

Use your teacher signal (key phrase or hand in air) to gain your students' attention. Give your directions clearly to help get assignments passed up. Set a time limit for completing this task.

> "Please put your novels away now and get out your math notebooks and pencils. I would like you to be ready in two minutes."

A large egg timer works as a great visual reminder. Just turn it over on your desk when you ask students to prepare for the next subject and ask them to be ready when the timer runs out.

As students are putting things away and getting supplies out for the next lesson, walk around the room and use your proximity or a hand on a desk to encourage any student who is slow in packing up. As a verbal cue and reminder, make a point of acknowledging either individuals or groups of students who are ready and waiting:

> "I see that the group of students by the blackboard has put their art projects on the shelf and have brought their gym bags to their desks. Thank you."

While work is being collected or materials are being put away, use the time to explain what the class will be doing next. Because you are giving directions during this changeover, they will have to listen carefully and move about the room quietly. Ask specific students to repeat your instructions for the class.

When students return from the gym or a specialist class, have their next assignment written on the board so that they can begin as soon as they come in. This is especially useful if you are teaching gym and are putting equipment away with a group of students or are rounding up stragglers in the changeroom. Also list any books or other materials students will need. Establish your expectations for those times when some students will be arriving in the classroom ahead of you. If students are not ready for this responsibility and choose to use this time inappropriately, request that they wait in the hallway until you arrive.

For that five minutes of time at the end of a lesson or when you are waiting for the arrival of a guest, keep on hand a book of riddles or puzzles that you can use to fill that short gap. Other options for those brief periods of time include reading from a

---

TRIED 'N TRUE

Practising math the fun way

For those longer periods of transition, you can teach students some math solitaire card games. These will also serve to reinforce basic facts and times tables. You can find a number of these in Margie Golick's *Reading, Writing, and Rummy*. You can post the directions for play somewhere in the room. This is an excellent opportunity to use peer tutors. You teach a small group of students a particular game, who in turn will teach others how to play. Send a note home to parents explaining the purpose of the cards when you request that each student bring an old deck from home. These card games are also an excellent way for students to practise those annoying facts and tables at home.

---

class novel or asking students to read from their own books that they keep in their desks for this purpose.

Handling Seating Arrangments

If students had their way, the majority of them would sit with their friends. This situation, of course, does not make for the most conducive learning environment!

With younger students, you will want to take the responsibility for deciding who will sit where, keeping in mind which students have attention problems as well as those who may need to sit close to the board due to vision problems.

With older students, select two to three students to form a committee responsible for designing the seating for one month. They can either draw up a blank seating plan, which you must then approve, or you can provide them with one of your blank plans. Using those cards numbered to match your class list, turn them face down, drawing one card at a time and putting that number in the first slot to be filled. They continue to draw numbers until all desks are assigned. Emphasize that they are to assign the numbers filling one grouping of desks before moving on to the next group. The seating plan must meet with your approval, so you will naturally check it to ensure that any behavior problems are strategically placed. The committee can then rearrange the desks after school when the majority of the students have gone. The students really enjoy this task!

Phys Ed Clothing

Your expectations regarding changing for phys ed may be influenced by school policy, facilities for changing, the length of phys ed periods, the age of your students, the type of activity, weather conditions, and, in some situations, religious restrictions. If you require students to change, stick to some stringent guidelines.

Safeguarding clothing. If students change in washrooms used by the whole school, have them bring their regular clothes into the gym or back to the classroom. Otherwise, student clothing left in washrooms will end up in urinals or toilets.

Time limits. Set a time limit for changing and begin your lesson regardless of whether all students are changed. A clock in each

Possible Seating Arrangements

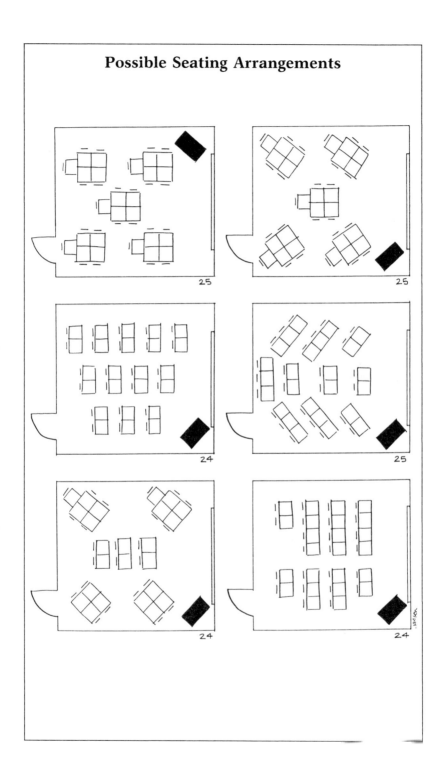

washroom is a great addition. Otherwise, how will they know? If there are no clocks, assign someone with a watch with the task of monitoring the time for the other students.

Making it fun. It will help matters if you always start with a fun warm-up activity. Would you rush to change just to do laps? They won't want to miss fun at the end of class either. If you send the slow changers to change early at the end of the lesson, they'll miss playing the final game. Students don't like missing out, so you will have provided an extra incentive to change more quickly next time.

Cleanliness. Have the students take their gym clothes home periodically throughout the year to be washed.

Remembering gym clothing. Forgotten gym clothes can be annoying. You may find that students do this deliberately to avoid phys ed. Keep a collection of clean but ugly T-shirts and make the forgetful ones wear them. They will also be expected to take the T-shirts home for washing before returning them.

WHAT THE EXPERTS SAY

"At the beginning of the school year, effective teachers showed evidence of careful planning and detailed thinking about procedures and student behavior in their classrooms. They planned routines that would help their classes function with a minimum of effort, and they had clear expectations for student behaviors in a wide array of classroom activities."*

WHAT THE EXPERTS SAY

"Teachers who devote three weeks at the beginning of the school year to establishing the procedures they deem necessary for smooth operations in their classrooms can thereby gain thirty-three weeks of efficient teaching."†

---

* Julie P. Sanford, Edmund T. Emmer, and Barbara S. Clements, "Improving Classroom Management," *Educational Leadership* (April 1983), p. 56
† "Effective Classroom Management Means More Time for Learning," *American Educator* (Summer 1984), p. 36. The author is commenting on a research study by Carolyn Evertson, Edwin Emmer, and Linda Anderson, *Beginning of the Year Classroom Management Study*, 1979.

3

Homework Routines

or

Keeping It Simple, Keeping You Sane

Well-designed homework assignments relate directly to classwork and extend students' learning beyond the classroom. Homework is most useful when teachers carefully prepare the assignment, thoroughly explain it, and give prompt comments and criticism when the work is completed.*

Homework Policies

Homework policy from school district to school district, from school to school, and from grade to grade can vary greatly. If you haven't done so already, find out from your administration what guidelines have been established for your teaching situation. These guidelines should cover several items of concern: the amount of homework assigned each day, the frequency with which homework can be assigned (e.g., daily or three times per week), types of homework, and school expectations of parents.

Ideally, all these concerns will have been clearly defined; however, this may not be the case. If these issues are left to the

---

* William J. Bennett, Secretary, *What Works: Research About Teaching and Learning*, second edition (United States Department of Education, 1987), p. 53

teacher's discretion, it is up to you to develop your own classroom guidelines. *NOTE: Make sure you inform and discuss your classroom homework policy with the administration. There may be "unwritten" rules about such issues as amount of homework or consequences for forgotten homework. If you run into unwritten rules, tactfully suggest that a school homework policy would be helpful.*

Homework Routines

A number of proven homework routines can help you ensure that homework assignments are understood and completed on time.

Reminder book. Implement a homework logbook or daily reminder book. These are produced commercially or you can design your own format. Students can use these calendars on a daily basis for recording their assignments — an excellent reminder technique. If you design your own, be sure to include a space for parent or teacher comments (encouraging continuing parent/school communication). The best commercially produced student calendars include extras, such as challenging word and number problems, a pocket for worksheets, a section on goal setting with space to record monthly goals, a book log, a list of most-misspelled words, a space to record problem words, and math problem-solving strategies. Canadian teachers should keep in mind that calendars published in Canada may also include such important tidbits as the words to "O Canada," Canadian holidays, and math references in metric. Premier School Agendas Ltd. produces an excellent elementary school reminder. As well, this company produces a large laminated homework chart set up to coordinate with the pages of the student homework book.

Collecting homework books. At the beginning of each day, collect approximately one-fifth of the homework books. Then you won't be faced with 30 books to write in at one sitting. Assign a day to each group of students and establish the expectation that the homework book will be placed on your desk as they arrive on that morning. During the day, write a brief message to parents regarding their child's performance or behavior over the past five days. These comments will prove invaluable during report-card time and interviews. The following are samples of comments:

"Jennifer did a great job of solving our math stumper this week. It was a tough one. Congratulations!"

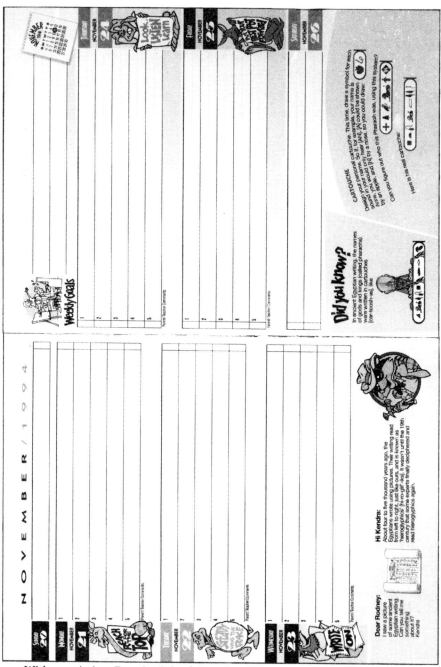

With permission: Premier School Agendas, "Elementary Reminder," (original in color)

"Excellent score on division post-test. 24/25!"

"Jeff is making a real effort to cooperate with others. Well done!"

"Mary needs to continue reviewing her basic facts each night for 5-10 minutes."

Reminders. Use the last ten minutes of class to review homework and allow students to record homework in the logbook. Post homework on a large chart clearly visible to all students. This gives the slow writers an opportunity to finish copying the assignment at their own pace. Display a sample of the worksheet assigned for homework by hanging it from a cup hook beside the homework chart. A visual reminder helps! Spot-check a few students to see that they have recorded homework properly.

Home study area. Develop and communicate to parents and students basic guidelines regarding the study area. An appropriate desk should be set aside for this purpose and equipped with supplies that should remain at home. These should include writing utensils and paper. Emphasize the importance of establishing a daily homework time.

On-going assignments. As well as assigning specific homework, have available for parents and students a list of on-going activities that could be undertaken to augment your work in the classroom. These

---

TRIED 'N TRUE

A ticket system for homework

Try the following system if you teach the lower grades: The teacher gives out the homework assignment for the week on Monday, in such subjects as math or spelling. Although the assignment is due on Friday, students who hand in their homework before Friday receive a ticket. After they have collected a set number of tickets they receive a small reward. The teacher records the date that the child hands in his or her homework. If homework is returned on Friday, the date is recorded but no ticket is given. Those who forget their homework on Friday either stay after school to finish, using extra sheets that the teacher has kept for that purpose, or the parent is contacted and asked to make sure that the work is done over the weekend. The remainder of the class has no homework assigned on the weekend.

activities can be specific for the student who has a weakness in a particular area. These could include silent reading for a certain time period each night, times-tables practice with flashcards, or review of spelling words from a personal word list.

Making it easy. For your own sake, assign easy-to-mark homework. You may also have the students mark their own or each other's homework, spot-checking a few students or marking a few questions from each student's work.

The Importance of Homework

Ensure that all homework assignments are based on concepts and processes already taught in the classroom. This increases the possibility that the student can complete the assignment independently. Remember that practice helps students learn what you have taught them. Practice and reinforcement should be the main purpose of the homework you assign.

When you find yourself swamped with homework assignments that should have been marked two days ago and plagued by excuses for lost and forgotten homework, you may ask yourself "Why bother?" Well, it *is* worthwhile. Just keep in mind what the experts say:

> Effective homework assignments do not just supplement the classroom lesson; they also teach students to be independent learners. Homework gives students experience in following directions, making judgments and comparisons, raising additional questions for study, and developing responsibility and self-discipline.[*]

and

> Student achievement rises significantly when teachers regularly assign homework and students conscientiously do it.[†]

SUGGESTION: Lee Cantor has written a series of books all about homework that are both theoretically sound and practical. They include Homework Without Tears, Practice Homework, Homework

---

[*] William J. Bennett, Secretary, *What Works: Research About Teaching and Learning,* second edition (United States Department of Education, 1987), p 53
[†] Ibid., p. 51

Motivators, *and* Creative Homework. *The first book has two versions, one for parents and the other for teachers. The remaining three titles also have two versions, one for Grades 1–3 and one for Grades 4–6.*

Forgotten or Incomplete Homework

I'm sure you've heard it all, including, "Honest. The dog ate it!" Consequences need to be established for both forgetting homework and not completing homework. These consequences will vary according to grade level, transportation situation, and extracurricular activities but should be established and adhered to.

The consequences you choose are endless. I'll outline a few appropriate ones. First, you can make a note of the transgression in the student homework book. The student will have to show his or her parents and have them initial the homework book.

A second approach is to oversee the completion of the work. If students aren't bussed, you can have them stay after school the following day to complete the next homework assignment.

If the problem continues, you can always phone the parents to discuss the situation or arrange for an interview at which the student is expected to be present.

Discuss with your students the importance of homework for developing their problem-solving abilities. As a class, brainstorm possible solutions for the following situations:

Textbook at school
- Borrow textbook from classmate.
- Come to school early enough to do homework before school.
- Go over to classmate's house and share textbook.

Worksheet at school
- Phone classmate, who can dictate questions.
- Go over to classmate's house if he or she hasn't done the homework yet and use his or her sheet to copy from.
- Go to school early.

Forgot to copy down assignment
- Phone classmate.
- Go to school early.

Forgot to bring homework back

- Once homework is complete, put in school pack, in sleeve of jacket, or in lunch bag immediately after completion.

4

Setting the Stage for Learning
or
A Foundation for Student Success

To become successful learners, students must first comprehend that they play the most crucial role in the process. Active learners are aware of their responsibilities and rights, understand the need for consequences if they misbehave, and establish realistic goals for themselves. Perhaps this was the greatest single fault of education in the past — reducing it to the content-oriented three Rs rather than focusing on strategies and skills. By setting the stage for learning, we, as teachers, show the students the road to success.

Rules, Rights, and Responsibilities

Times have changed. With the larger, more demanding classes of today, one could say that the three Rs have changed from reading, 'riting, and 'rithmetic to rules, rights, and responsibilities.

Your school will have certain rules by which all students must abide, so learn these and go over them carefully with your class at the beginning of the year. Post them in the classroom.

Within the classroom, you will have more flexibility, but in order to establish a healthy working atmosphere and to foster ownership in the classroom, the following two strategies have proven successful. Either process will take more time than simply posting teacher-imposed rules but will create a totally different tone in your classroom. Most important, these strategies will place the responsibility for student behavior in the hands of the students. For either of the two formats, begin with a short discussion of the differences between rights, privileges, and responsibilities:

- RIGHTS: something we are entitled to
- PRIVILEGES: something we have earned
- RESPONSIBILITIES: something that is expected of us by others

Emphasis on Rights*
To introduce the topic, display or pass out a copy of the United Nations Declaration of the Rights of the Child. Emphasize that, in our country, many of these rights are taken for granted, yet in other parts of the world children are denied these rights.

United Nations Declaration
of
The Rights of the Child

- The right to affection, love, and understanding.
- The right to adequate nutrition and medical care.
- The right to protection against all forms of neglect, cruelty, and exploitation.
- The right to free education and to full opportunity for play and recreation.
- The right to a name and nationality.
- The right to special care, if handicapped.
- The right to be among the first to receive relief in times of disaster.
- The right to learn to be a useful member of society and to develop individual abilities.
- The right to learn to be a useful member of society and to develop individual abilities.
- The right to be brought up on a spirit of peace and universal brotherhood.
- The right to enjoy these rights, regardless of race, color, sex, religion, national or social origin.

(1979)

---

*With permission: This students' rights activity has been adapted from one that appeared in the Calgary Board of Education's *Family Life Curriculum*.

Divide the class into small groups and have them brainstorm a list of student rights, though they cannot overrule either existing school rules or existing guidelines, such as the length of the school day and the need to work within the framework of subjects specified by the Department of Education. Make sure you circulate from group to group to monitor ideas and make suggestions.

At the end of 10 to 15 minutes, compile a class set of rights by taking an item from each group in turn, until all rights are listed. Be prepared to reword some statements and allow discussion. You may need to regroup ideas if some statements are similar in intent.

A note of caution: Older students may attempt to push the limits of what is acceptable in a school setting, so it may be necessary to emphasize what their responsibilities are when attending school. Remind them that these are not open to negotiation. Print the final draft on chart paper and post it in the classroom.

Samples of Students' Rights

(Compiled by Grade 4 and 6 Students)

I HAVE A RIGHT TO
1. be an individual.
2. keep my own property and privacy.
3. be treated equally.
4. speak without being interrupted.
5. be heard.
6. be safe and comfortable.
7. not be disturbed when doing my work.
8. interesting and challenging lessons.
9. express my feelings.
10. be treated with respect.
11. ask questions.
12. make mistakes without being criticized.
13. be treated equally by teachers.
14. my own friends, but to treat all classmates kindly.
15. learn to the best of my ability.

Emphasis on Responsibility

To begin this approach, develop a list of synonyms for the word "responsibility," including such words as "commitment," "duty," and "expectation." At this point you may well want to focus on the concept of who we are responsible to and why.

Divide the class into small groups and invite them to brainstorm a list of student responsibilities, though this list must not contradict established school rules and guidelines, as outlined above. Once again, make sure you move from group to group listening and encouraging. At the end of 10 to 15 minutes, compile a class set of student responsibilities. Allow for discussion and reorganization of ideas.

The following day, follow the same procedure to produce a list of teacher responsibilities. You may wish to give some input when you reach the stage where you are compiling a class list. Students may be unaware of some of the expectations that the principal, school board, department of education, and parents have regarding your job.

On the third day, establish a list of parent responsibilities.

Compile the three lists and make copies to send home for parent/guardian feedback. Parents usually cooperate quite willingly, happy to see this sort of exercise. You may find that you're encouraging some interesting dialogue between parent and child.

Once any last changes from parents have been recorded and discussed within the class, the three components should be copied onto chart paper and posted so they are easily visible to all students. It becomes very easy to make reference to an individual item when a student has forgotten his or her responsibilities and infringed upon a classmate's or your rights.

NOTE: Whatever format you use, discuss with the class the relationship between rights and responsibilities. Use examples from your chart; for example, if a student has the right not to be disturbed when doing his or her work, then other students' have the responsibility to let him or her work undisturbed. With older students, introduce the idea of approving either of the final documents through a formal motion. This is an ideal topic for the agenda of an early classroom meeting.

Samples of Parent, Teacher, and Student Responsibilities

(Compiled by Grade 4 Students and Their Parents)

PARENT RESPONSIBILITIES
1. Make sure we are dressed properly.
2. Make sure we are well rested.
3. Listen to our problems.
4. Give us healthy meals.
5. Be fair and honest.
6. Help us with our homework if we need it and provide a suitable work place for us to work in.
7. Spend time with us.
8. Have a sense of humour.
9. Give us praise and encouragement.
10. Encourage us to become independent. Don't overprotect us.

TEACHER RESPONSIBILITIES
1. Be organized.
2. Make sure we behave properly.
3. Be fair and honest.
4. Teach to each student's ability.
5. Make sure we understand the lessons.
6. Smile. Be cheerful and happy.
7. Do not overwork us.
8. Have a sense of humor.
9. If one of us does something wrong, don't punish all of us.
10. Do not punish one of us in front of the rest of the class.

STUDENT RESPONSIBILITIES
1. Respect other people.
2. Be fair and honest.
3. Work your hardest.
4. Always listen when someone is talking.
5. Respect other people's property.
6. Obey school rules.
7. Do your homework on time.
8. Raise your hand when you wish to speak.
9. Think before you speak. Think before you act.
10. Treat others as they would like to be treated.

The Discipline Dilemma

Losing control of a class is every teacher's worst nightmare. If you can't control their behavior, you can't teach. The issue of discipline or lack of it in schools continues to be the education topic that generates the most discussion in the media. Not surprisingly, this issue causes great concern among teachers and is often cited as a prime reason for teachers leaving the profession. Although the picture painted is often gloomy, take heart in the fact that many teachers have developed systems of classroom management that minimize the discipline problems in their classrooms.

To a large degree, the key is PREVENTION. And the key to prevention is, you guessed it, PREPARATION. To prepare adequately, you must clarify all school rules and establish cooperatively with your students the rights and responsibilities of students, teacher, and parents. You must define any procedures and routines that will provide for the smooth running of the classroom. In communicating all of this, you will eliminate most of the misbehaviors that arise when students don't know the parameters under which your classroom operates.

Discipline Dos

The following are a number of strategies you can employ to help keep your classroom manageable. After all, none of us likes to hear ourselves barking, "Stop that now!... I said '*now*'!"

Establish right at the beginning of the year that the teacher and students share common goals and are working as a team. You can then avoid the unfortunate stereotype of the teacher as authoritarian who must take full responsibility for control of the classroom.

Be your most strict at the beginning of the year. Many an experienced teacher has horror stories of their first year, when they decided that being a friend to the students would eliminate the need for any discipline. And so they began the year with a very relaxed attitude. Result: chaos! Remember, it is much easier to give more freedom to students once they have proven they can handle it than to impose authority on an unruly group. One young student reflects on her teacher's yo-yo-like disciplinary tactics: "At first you were fun, then you were mean. Now you have discipline."

Use visual references around the classroom. Copies of school rules, classroom rights, and procedures for getting drinks, handing up work, and leaving the classroom will all reinforce and remind students of your expectations. Another invaluable addition to your classroom wall would be a list of monthly classroom goals. (See page 59.)

Emphasize that when a student chooses to misbehave, he or she has also chosen to accept the consequences for his or her decision. The responsibility is the student's, and you are simply respecting his or her decision. Be sure to use the word "consequence" rather than "punishment."

Establish reasonable and logical consequences for any misbehavior. The consequence for something minor, such as going for a drink while the teacher is talking, could be the loss of water fountain privileges for that student for the remainder of the day. For a more serious situation, such as swearing or "talking back" to the teacher, you may wish to speak to the student privately, give the student "time out" in the cloakroom, or phone the parents. As an alternative, have the student explain his or her behavior in a note that must be taken home, signed by the parent or guardian, and returned to the teacher.

Take into account whether the misbehavior is a first-time occurrence or not. If the student consistently behaves in an unacceptable manner after a first consequence has been used, then you may need to impose a more serious consequence.

It always helps to keep tabs on the mood of your class. If you notice the students fidgeting, give them an opportunity to get out of their desks and stretch. If a number of them are talking out of turn, especially while you are working with one student or a group, refocus their behavior by referring to your chart of responsibilities before the noise gets out of hand. If you notice a "situation" developing, often the use of physical proximity and a question regarding their work will be enough to diffuse any potential problems.

Be consistent in both your expectations and in your application of consequences. Consistency creates a "comfort level," which provides security to your students and defines your role. This is not to say that you can never be flexible. Sometimes you must take extenuating circumstances into account, such as a recent family crisis.

Consider the causes of misbehavior. Your remedies may vary depending on the origin of the behavior. Ask yourself:

- Is the student seeking attention?
- Is the student attention deficit?
- Could the student be bored with the work because it is not challenging enough for his or her ability?
- Could the student be frustrated with the work because he or she does not understand the concepts or instructions?
- Is the student finished his or her work and unable to decide what to do next?
- Is the student highly active and having trouble concentrating?
- Or is the student merely challenging authority by behaving in an uncooperative, defiant manner?

In all instances, the remedy will involve some modification to your classroom organization.

The attention seeker may need to be given a place to work where he or she won't disturb others. Place the desk in a location that physically separates the student from the rest of the class. You might also restrict the student's movement by requiring the child to ask permission to leave his or her desk. These tactics will alleviate the situation in most cases.

The attention-deficit (AD) student may need both a relatively non-distracting work area and assistance in monitoring and increasing his or her attention span. Much has been written on the management of AD children. Depending on the severity of the disorder, this problem may require a concerted effort on your part to be consistent and objective in your day-to-day dealings with these students, who often tax your patience and wear you down. Keep in mind that their behaviors are often beyond their control.

The student who is bored by the level of work assigned should have his or her individual needs met through some form of enrichment or condensing of units.

The student frustrated by the difficulty of work also requires some program modification to bring the material to a level at which he or she can work independently. It is your responsibility to meet the individual needs of students at both ends of the spectrum.

For students who are finished their work quickly, you can provide other meaningful activities for them to pursue once they have checked their work carefully and followed any procedures regarding handing their work up. Once again, it is the teacher's responsibility to provide activities and establish guidelines. Your students will find it helpful if you display a list that indicates the options available.

The highly active student requires more frequent changes of pace and extra feedback from the teacher to keep him or her on task. Breaking an assignment into smaller "chunks," which offer the opportunity for short breaks in between, will help.

The defiant student is the most difficult to deal with because it is so difficult to pin down the possible reason for the continual challenge to the smooth running of the classroom. Often circumstances outside the school have contributed to this student's seemingly deliberate and uncooperative actions. You may need to resort to a behavior contract or discipline plan.

NOTE: There are a number of valuable resources available to guide you in your dealings with these students. Lee Canter's Assertive Discipline *and* Succeeding With Difficult Children, *and* You Can Handle Them All *from The Master Teacher are but a few that may be of help.*

Discipline Don'ts

To maintain control, you will have to make sure you don't commit any of the many discipline don'ts. You will find these are sometimes hard to avoid, especially when your patience is strained to the limit. Be careful. To avoid making mistakes you'll immediately regret, follow these rules:

- Never state a consequence or punishment on which you cannot follow through.
- Never make open-ended threats such as "... or else" or "You'll be sorry." These are vague and empty and will eventually carry no weight.
- Never call students names or insult them.
- Never show your frustration by becoming visibly emotional, that is, by yelling or crying.
- Never use any form of physical punishment, such as pinching, squeezing, or pulling.
- Never punish the whole class when the misbehavior is the responsibility of only a few.
- Never keep the whole class for a detention until someone "owns up." It rarely works and you'll just look foolish.
- Never allow a student to draw you into an argument or "war of words."

This last "never" can be difficult to avoid. Just remember that your word is final and discussion is not an option. Simply state that you will discuss the student's concern with him or her after school.

Monitoring Behavior

If more than one teacher instructs your students, you'll have to put in place some method for monitoring student behavior from teacher to teacher. Otherwise, discipline may be inconsistent and those students who are misbehaving in a number of classes will never be held accountable for their actions because of the lack of communication between teachers.

A class logbook is an effective means of keeping track of student behaviors throughout the day. Appoint a student to be responsible for carrying the logbook to any specialist classes and giving it to the teacher. At the end of that period, the teacher records a general comment about the class and notes the names of any students who have been disruptive, citing specific examples. At the end of the day, the homeroom teacher reads aloud the comments for the day and either praises the students for the nature of the comments or discusses with the class what can be done to improve behavior on the following day. If reference is made to an individual's behavior, the teacher should be prepared to follow up on the comments with the student concerned.

TRIED 'N TRUE

Reinforcing the behavior logbook

The class logbook is an excellent way of encouraging good behavior. Sometimes, however, you need reinforcement. Ask the principal to visit your class on a weekly or monthly basis — if he or she is not doing so already. Ask him or her to review the logbook in your students' presence and either congratulate the class members on their behavior or reinforce your efforts at dealing with any problems. Prior to the visit, notify the principal of any pressing issues and ensure that he or she understands your approach in any areas of concern. The last thing you need is contradiction!

Goal Setting

Self-esteem can be greatly enhanced by the achievement of a goal, no matter how small. The "I did it!" feeling is a great boost to self-confidence, which sets the stage for further successes. By implementing goal setting in your classroom, you can greatly improve your students' chances of success. Having goals or objectives to work toward, whether short term or long term, provides direction and enables students to focus their energy constructively. Goal setting places the onus of responsibility for attaining these goals where it belongs: on the student. That is not to say the teacher is "passing the buck." Instead it implies that achievement of goals is a cooperative effort in which the teacher facilitates, encourages, monitors, and assists the students in attaining their goals.

A number of factors should be considered before beginning the process of goal setting. The age of students, the types of goals to be set (e.g., academic, personal, or work habits), the usefulness of time limits, the method of monitoring, and the evaluation procedure used will all influence the success of this facet of classroom management.

To introduce the topic, begin by asking the students to offer their definition of a "goal." Most of them will think in terms of sports and define it as something for which you aim. This description works well because you can continue the analogy:

GOALS IN SPORTS	GOALS IN LIFE
• A goal in sports is close or far away.	• Any goal you set is either short or long term.
• On a sports field, you can move toward a goal because you know what it looks like.	• All goals are measurable.
• Players from the opposite team always try to stop you from reaching the goal.	• You always encounter obstacles in your pursuit of something.
• When you score, you feel great.	• When you achieve other goals, you feel great, too.
• Scoring pleases the fans.	• Achieving goals pleases your parents and teachers.
• If you miss the goal, you can try again.	• You can rephrase your goal, and try and try again!

Early Years

Students as young as five or six years of age can be taught to set goals. Tying shoelaces, putting supplies away, bringing library books back on time, or keeping desks tidy are all concrete tasks that can easily be reinforced and monitored by the teacher. If you keep in mind a few hints, you will help your students succeed and feel good about themselves.

- Always set short-term goals for young children.
- Post some visible cues, such as a picture or set of key words printed on a card, either on their desks or on a bulletin board.
- Use a stamp or mini-stickers to record evidence of your students' successes on a personal card. This allows the student to keep track of their progress.
- Make parents aware of their child's goals so they can offer support and encouragement as well.
- At the end, when a goal has been achieved, always present some form of recognition, such as a personal certificate.

Remember — and remind your students — there is no such thing as failure, only degrees of success. If a student needs more practice or time with a particular goal, you can either repeat the exercise immediately with a modification to the wording or set it aside till later in the year. The latter will be necessary if you see that the student has become frustrated or that, at this point in time, the goal is unrealistic for the child.

Middle Years

For older students, goal setting becomes even more important because of the increased expectations and responsibilities placed on them by both school and home.

Explaining. Begin by explaining the purpose of goal setting and that goal setting is a life-long strategy used by adults. Give examples of goals you have set for yourself both professionally and personally.

Determining the goal. Brainstorm possible goals under the following categories: academic goals, work-habit goals, and personal goals. You should first emphasize that goals must be realistic, specific, and measurable. The phrase ''to become better at spelling in daily work'' is both vague and difficult to assess. Suggest, instead, a more specific goal: ''to proofread any written

Samples of Individual Student Goals

(Collected by Grade 4-6 Students)

WORK HABITS
1. Raise my hand when I want to speak.
2. Work without disturbing others.
3. Listen to directions from teacher.
4. Keep my mind on my work until I'm finished.
5. Proofread my work carefully.
6. Get started quickly.
7. Do corrections promptly.
8. Be neat in daily work.
9. Be organized (desk, binders, supplies.)
10. Use any spare time wisely.

ACADEMIC
1. Study for weekly spelling tests.
2. Read for half an hour every night.
3. Be more neat in handwriting.
4. Learn my basic facts for addition.
5. Improve my scores on times-tables tests.
6. Return homework on time.
7. Use capitals and punctuation consistently.
8. Improve my word processing skills.
9. Read math problems carefully.
10. Check for careless errors on tests.

PERSONAL
1. Be on time for school.
2. Think for myself, don't let others think for me.
3. Get along better with my sister.
4. Keep my room clean.
5. Try not to get into fights at recess.
6. Watch less TV.
7. Try not to bite my nails.
8. Do my chores without being reminded.
9. Do my homework before watching TV.
10. Get along with my parents — don't argue.

NOTE: Samples of student-developed goals are invaluable when working with your class on goal setting, especially the first time. Refer to this list after your class has brainstormed their own collection of goals.

assignments twice and refer to a dictionary for any spellings I'm unsure of."

Setting the parameters. After developing a healthy list of possible goals, allow the children to choose a limited number of goals for themselves. Help them determine the length of time within which they should achieve their goals. This may vary from a month to a year. If goals are long term, ensure that monitoring occurs on a regular basis such as biweekly or monthly

Encouraging. Establish visual cues for each student. A goal statement and record may be kept on a card attached to the student's desk or on a piece of looseleaf paper in the front of his or her binder. You should also make a point of referring to the students' goals on a consistent basis. Invite them to read their goal statements silently and ask themselves how they are doing. Plan brief individual conferences while students are doing seatwork to discuss the child's progress. It helps to inform parents of their child's goals, requesting their support.

Keeping track. Develop a simple system that the students can use for rating their progress. Any system that works on a continuum will make it easier for the student to assess what stage he or she is at. A five-point rating or anecdotal rating using phrases such as "There," "Almost There," "Getting There," and "Nowhere Near There" is sufficient to help students self-evaluate. Using the same system as the students chose, provide an evaluation for each student and a short conference to discuss any problems or discrepancies with his or her evaluation.

Class Goal Setting

Working toward common goals can really develop a class's cohesiveness and cooperative focus, as well as provide a positive approach to classroom management.

Begin each new month with a discussion of possible classroom goals based on seasonal situations as well as problems that have arisen during the previous month. Select two or three classroom goals. You can also choose a "service goal," which can be directed within the school or the community. Such activities as volunteer work for a home for seniors or a day-care centre, or fund raising in order to purchase something for either group, can be very rewarding and will encourage your students to think of the needs of others.

Record the goals on a laminated chart that you can post in a clearly visible spot. Refer to the chart throughout the month, drawing students' attention to their goals if you notice them "slacking off." At the end of the month, have them show with the five-finger method how well they think they scored as a class. If the majority of students show a rating of three or less, discuss possible reasons and alternative approaches to improve the score.

Samples of Monthly Classroom Goals

1. Make ____ (new student's name) feel welcome in our class.
2. Remain calm and civilized during the Christmas season.
3. Use capital letters consistently.
4. Behave responsibly when leaving the classroom for washroom visits.
5. Raise your hand when you want to speak.
6. When working with a partner or a group, use your quiet voice.
7. Remember to take home all notices and newsletters.
8. Be ready when the second bell rings.
9. Use transition time wisely.
10. Remember to reduce, reuse, and recycle.

If the majority rate the class as a four or more, consider the goal to have been achieved. Encourage everyone to congratulate each other. A small reward or celebration, such as extending their recess by 5 minutes or granting them 15 minutes of free time at the end of the day, is appropriate.

NOTE: If you have access to a speaker such as an athlete or author whose message relates to the importance of setting goals for success in life, by all means make use of them. They will serve to drive home the relevance of what you have been working on in school.

5

General Home-and-School Communication

or

A One-Way Street

There was a time, many years ago, when parent-teacher communication simply referred to the ominous report card filled with somewhat meaningless numbers and letters accompanied by a brief, cryptic comment. This was sent home three or four times a year and subsequently returned with either an authentic or forged signature from the parent, depending on the contents.

Well, we've come a long way since then and for good reason. In times past, though the home and school supposedly shared the responsibility of meeting the academic, social, emotional, and physical needs of each child, there was certainly no meeting of the minds on who was doing what and when it was being done.

As a classroom teacher, you should always take a positive, proactive approach to parent interest and involvement. Parents' concern about what happens to their child while under your care and supervision can be used to the child's benefit. Opening lines of communication, both formal and informal, can only serve to contribute to each child's total education and therefore make your task easier in the long run. It will also send a clear message to the child that both parents and the teacher care.

The simplest level of home-and-school communication can be categorized as one-way communication from the school to the parents as a group. By providing information about the school and classroom activities, you bring the parent into the school community. Group communication may include school hand-books, meet-the-teacher nights, regular newsletters, and school open houses.

The School Handbook

Most schools produce an annual school handbook that it sends home to each family at the beginning of the year. Typically, the handbook may include or describe the following:

- school staff and their assignments
- map of the building
- specialist programs
- parent-volunteer opportunities
- school year calendar
- school policies relating to absenteeism, homework, attendance, medications, and accidents that occur on school property
- standardized testing program
- awards program
- school rules
- reporting and interview procedures
- timetable of the school day
- lunch program

Take the time to familiarize yourself with the contents of the handbook. Parents will be asking you questions regarding the contents and will expect you to interpret anything unclear to them.

Meet-the-Teacher Night

This important but sometimes stressful event usually takes place during the first month of school. The purpose of this general meeting is to provide an overview of your classroom manage-ment procedures and to get acquainted with everyone. Here is your first opportunity to introduce yourself and to meet the parents of your students. This initial personal contact will allow you, in future, to put a face to the name.

Meet-the-teacher nights can be stressful because we all know the value of first impressions. In addition, you may well be expected to do a short presentation in your classroom to explain such topics as homework expectations, discipline policy, and specific classroom procedures. You may also be asked to present some form of curriculum content outline.

If your principal really wants to see you squirm, you and your colleagues will probably be introduced to the entire gathering of parents in the gym.

Try not to think of this evening as a "trial by fire." Put yourself in the parents' place. The majority of them are somewhat overwhelmed by visits to the school, memories of their schooling likely being less than positive, so you can be assured that they approach this first meeting with their child's teacher with an equal level of stress.

Your aim, on these meeting nights, is to put the parents at ease regarding two basic concerns. First, you need to assure parents that you are a competent teacher. You can best demonstrate this through the quality of your presentation and the displays around your room. If parents see that you have addressed a variety of topics and have visual displays to remind and reinforce them throughout your classroom, they will feel confident in your ability to teach the content prescribed and to provide an environment that is both caring and predictable for their child.

The second concern you should address on this meet-the-teacher night is your *approachability*. Parents must know that they can contact you if a concern arises. Specify methods by which this can be done: sending notes, making phone calls, and stopping by the classroom after teaching hours. Do set some parameters regarding these methods. If you are comfortable with phone calls to your home, then by all means give out your home number. If not, indicate that they can leave a message with the office and you will return their call as soon as you are available. Unscheduled visits to the classroom are suitable as long as you are not teaching at the time. If they can call ahead of time and indicate the specific concern they wish to discuss with you, it will give you an opportunity to prepare and reflect upon the issue. *NOTE: In some schools, especially large urban facilities, visitors are expected to check in with the office prior to visiting a classroom. Check on your school policy and inform parents of the policy.*

To prepare for this special evening, you should undertake a number of tasks. A week or so ahead of time, the students can design invitations for their parents. Even the younger students can draw a picture on the front of a computer-generated invitation. On the day of the event, ask your students to clean out their desks thoroughly, as well as tidy up the cloakroom. Some parents will check their child's desk on meet-the-teacher night, and they're sure to "see red" if it is as messy as their child's room!

Prepare a concise handout that outlines your homework policy. Be sure to include the details regarding forgotten homework as well as homework that is not completed. Suggest that this handout be kept at home near the child's study area or on one of those family bulletin boards as a reminder.

Prepare a short talk during which you can outline your classroom procedures and routines. Parents should already be aware of the student, teacher, and parent responsibilities if you used this strategy for establishing behavioral guidelines. If you and your students generated a list of student rights during the first week, it is important to refer to them.

Have ready to distribute a list of art supplies you would like students to bring from home if they can.

If you are expected to inform parents of curriculum expectations for your grade, either have a handout ready or prepare a chart or transparency. Try to include examples of the various objectives so that parents aren't confused by educational jargon.

Keep in mind that the purpose of this evening is to provide an overview of your classroom-management procedures and to get acquainted with everyone. It is not the time to discuss individual student problems or parent concerns regarding school policies or rules. Suggest that such issues are best dealt with through a conference scheduled for a later date. Phrases such as "Let's continue this discussion at another time when there's not so many people around," or "I'd like some time to look through _____'s folder before I comment on his/her progress," are useful. If all else fails, start packing up your things and move toward the door of your room!

Monthly Newletters

Many schools prepare a monthly newsletter to bring parents up to date on special events that have occurred during the previous month as well as to inform them of any up-and-coming events that will affect the whole school. These may include guest speakers, fund raising activities, field trips, parent advisory council meetings, survey results, requests for volunteers, or notification of professional development days.

A class newsletter is an effective way to keep parents informed of what's happening in your classroom. It can be sent home weekly, biweekly, monthly, or sporadically. With the lower grades, the majority of its contents can be prepared by you with verbal input from the students. Including student work in the newsletter is an excellent idea, providing that you keep track of whose work is spotlighted each month — you must ensure that everyone has a turn.

In the upper grades, the newsletter can be totally prepared by the students. Remember that a student-prepared newsletter is much more likely to make it home than one prepared exclusively by you! Begin by brainstorming to generate the contents, and then establish groups to prepare a short "blurb" on each topic. To save time, you should have a blank newsletter column format to use, so that you or one of the groups can then cut and paste to prepare a finished copy ready for photocopying.

TRIED 'N TRUE

Getting the newsletter home

To ensure that a newsletter actually makes it home, a "Safe Arrival of the Newsletter" box works quite well. In one corner of the newsletter, design a small box requesting the parents' acknowledgment of receipt. After being signed, this portion is returned by the child to the class or the office and put into a cardboard box designated for this purpose. Approximately a week later, one or two names are drawn from this collection and the lucky students get to select a prize. Inexpensive but useful items such as erasers or colorful pencils prove very popular.

Public Education Weeks

The purpose of an education week is to provide information on tax-supported education to the tax-paying general public. The dates for these events are usually designated by either upper level administration or the teachers' association. Usually these weeks are granted a broad theme, such as "Educating for Tomorrow."

Individual schools may choose to set a more specific focus for the week's events. Highlighting a specific subject area and planning a variety of classroom-based as well as cross-grade events is a common format. Taking education out into the community by getting permission from businesses and stores to set up displays of student projects is an innovative approach to gaining public exposure and support for education.

An "Open House" evening is frequently scheduled during this week, which provides the school with another opportunity to invite the parents into the school. At one time, an open house simply involved pinning up good copies of student writing and art projects on bulletin boards. Parents wandered through the school, occasionally stopping to read a poem or story, and, as soon as feasible, excused themselves.

Nowadays, it is more common to see parents involved in learning by doing. This entails some effort on the staff's part to set up activity centres for the parents. Here are three examples of themes and activity-centre ideas:

- "Math is All Around Us" would feature math problem-solving activities based on everyday situations. Opportunities to record answers and draw names for prizes is certainly an option.
- "The World at Play" would involve physical games as well as board games from around the world.
- "Stretch Your Thinking" lends itself to any sort of riddle, puzzle, or brainstorming activity. Visitors could be challenged to record unusual uses for everyday objects or undertake fluency activities such as thinking of various phrases using the same word, e.g., "bear."

These centres can be located in the hallway and the gym as well as in classrooms. Use of common areas is less intimidating to some parents and will encourage them to mingle and talk with a greater variety of people, rather than just the parents of students in their child's class.

Miscellaneous Presentations

A variety of informal classroom activities and projects serve as excellent means of providing feedback to parents regarding the on-going learning in your classroom. The majority are performance-oriented, and so will motivate the parent to attend. These include class plays, poetry readings, art shows, and displays of science projects. An anthology of student writing, selected and compiled by students, serves as an excellent class project as well as providing the student with a memento he or she will treasure.

Presentations produce a number of obvious and not-so-obvious benefits. By providing a variety of opportunities for parents to visit the classroom and school on an informal basis, you increase their comfort level with education in general and you in particular.

By providing an audience for your students, you increase their motivation to produce a first-rate finished product — it's not just another assignment to be handed in to the teacher and consequently forgotten. Concepts of polishing and editing a product can be easily reinforced.

By providing an opportunity for parents to see their child in action, they will have a clearer picture of how their child behaves in social situations with peers. They will also see how their child compares to other children academically and socially. These observations offer valuable information for parents and allow them to draw some conclusions regarding their child's progress rather than relying solely on your evaluations.

By organizing "shared experiences," the parents, child, and you will have something to discuss during interview time. You can also glean some interesting insights into the child of which you might otherwise be unaware. And in some small way, you might counteract the negative images of education as it is portrayed in the media.

6

One-on-One Home-and-School Communication

or

A Two-Way Street

Communication between home and school involves more than the one-way divulgence of general information from the school to the parents. You may have to use your imagination to generate effective two-way communication. Besides good old-fashioned report cards, you can try homework-book messages, good-news notes, phone calls, informal student feedback, and parent-student-teacher conferences.

Homework

Parents are a crucial backup for your efforts. You will need them to help make sure that homework gets done, so communicate to them your expectations. Request at the outset that they check the homework logbook at least once a week to read your comments and either initial the comment or write a message back to you. You will find that this becomes a quick and meaningful way to establish informal communication. Parents are quite appreciative of the day-to-day contact. This approach also lets the student know that his or her parents and teachers are consistent and informed — and that they care.

Communicate to parents that the student should be able to complete homework independently without a parent's assistance, and if such is not the case they should indicate this in the homework logbook. Set a time limit for homework. If a student is taking too long, the parents should let you know. Between you, it can then be determined if the problem is one of lack of understanding or inability to concentrate.

Good-News Notes

As teachers, our attention is often drawn to problem situations rather than to the many good things that happen every day in the classroom. Using good-news notes can make us more aware of our students' positive behaviors and achievements. Also, they bring happiness wherever they're sent.

A wide variety of commercially produced good-news notes are available by catalogue or from teacher stores. These usually relate to either achievement in a specific subject or positive behaviors. You simply fill in the blanks to produce a personal message, which you can send home to keep the parents informed. This type of concrete positive reinforcement works especially well with the lower grades. Young students take great pride in these messages and will often display them on a bulletin board in their room or on the fridge (thanks to fridge magnets). They require minimal time to complete and serve as yet another method of informal communication. With older students, a special message included in the homework book and shown to the student before sending home means a lot.

Phoning Home

Don't forget the quickest method of all. Phone calls are especially effective because you know for certain that the parents received the message. You also get immediate feedback regarding the information you are passing along. On the one hand, teachers often use the telephone if they have a serious concern regarding behavior or achievement or if there is a problem with homework. Try to present your bad-news information as objectively as possible and ask for the parents' cooperation in helping you resolve any problems. Negativity and laying of blame are immediate turnoffs!

On the other hand, "sunshine calls" can certainly brighten a parent's day. Parents don't usually expect these, however. They have been conditioned to believe that the only time a teacher wants to talk to them is when their child has done something wrong. Don't hesitate to call when a student has demonstrated extra effort on a project, cooperation with classmates, or helpfulness to you.

Regardless of the nature of the call, have a prepared sentence to begin, so that parents immediately know the purpose of the call. Here are some examples you might use:

"I'm just calling you to let you know I've congratulated _____ on _____."

"I'm calling because _____ has been _____ about _____. Could we get together to discuss this further?"

When you follow up on a parent conference, you may wish to initiate weekly or monthly "progress report" phone calls to address an issue that was brought up at the interview. It is amazing how motivated students become when they realize that their parents and teacher are in consistent communication with each other.

Informal Student Feedback

The classic comment offered in response to the oft asked question, "What did you do/learn in school today?" is, of course, "Nothing." How do you get around this dilemma?

The trick is to prepare your students immediately before they leave your classroom. Use that last five or ten minutes at the end of the day to have the students summarize or review what they learned that day. Initially, you may have to model for them so they understand what you mean. You can even invite them to record this information in their homework logbook. You may wish to send home samples of work, asking your students to have their parents initial the work to indicate that they have seen it.

Report Cards

Report-card time — a period of stress for all concerned! To you, the teacher, it means trying to crystallize your data and observations so that you can document every student's progress both accurately and succinctly while still preparing lessons, marking assignments, and carrying on with the normal classroom routines.

It also means preparing yourself to meet 25 or more sets of parents, to whom you will have to explain and justify the marks and comments permanently recorded about their child. No wonder most teachers look bleary eyed and exhausted by the time reports and conferences are finished!

To the child, report-card time can mean a sudden onslaught of last-minute tests and evaluations, anxious parents whose concern about marks seems totally out of proportion to the child's priorities, unwanted comparisons between siblings and peers by parents and other children, a teacher who seemingly has aged five years in the last month, and, worst of all, the knowledge that his or her abilities, achievements, attitudes, and behavior are all about to be revealed and discussed.

To the parents, report-card time once again harkens back to their own experiences in the school system. It can mean trying to read between the lines of unclear comments, wondering why schools are spending time teaching all those "frill" subjects, trying to interpret complicated marking systems, feeling frustrated with a child who doesn't seem to take his or her education seriously enough, worrying about their child's future, and fearing that their performance as parents will be called into question as a result of that daunting document.

All in all, it would seem better for all concerned if report cards went the way of the dodo bird! However, report cards are like taxes: nobody likes them but we can't live without them. The issue becomes a matter of how each stakeholder can make the best of the situation.

The teacher, as the professional, has the greatest responsibility to ensure that both parents and child receive meaningful and relevant feedback on the child's strengths and weaknesses. The keys to success and survival are, once again, planning and organization.

Schools and boards vary greatly in their guidelines regarding report cards. Report-card formats can vary greatly from school to school, and grade to grade:

- Totally anecdotal. No marks.
- Achievement and effort marks as well as anecdotal comments relating to both subject areas and work habits.
- Achievement and effort marks as well as a brief general comment.

Parent/teacher conference formats can also vary greatly:

- Optional: based upon teacher or parent request
- Inclusive: not considered compulsory but requested of all parents
- Student present: child included for at least part of the proceedings

At the Beginning of the Year

Preparing early will make your job much easier later on. To begin, familiarize yourself with your school's particular report-card format and grading system (if any). Also request a copy of the school's criteria used for assessing achievement and effort.

Open a file folder for each student in which you can compile unit tests, work samples, diagnostic test results, observations, behavioral checklists, and notes on any parent communications. At the same time, ask your students to prepare a portfolio: a folder into which they can put creative writing samples, selected journal entries, samples of math assignments, an audiotape of their oral reading, personal goals, social studies or science finished products, and favorite works of art.

Discuss with your students the types of assessments you will use throughout the year. Emphasize that tests are only one component. Everything counts: their assignments, their participation, their attitude — everything. It might be a sensible idea to explain to the students the purposes of assessment, and to clarify the difference between diagnostic and evaluative forms. Outline the grading system and the criteria that you will use. Emphasize that grades are earned not given, so the responsibility is theirs!

Throughout the Term

Generate and collect a wide variety of assessment information, such as checklists outlining mastery of subject-matter objectives, anecdotal comments regarding work habits and social skills, teacher-made test scores, student self-assessments, diagnostic test scores, standardized test scores, resource room/counselling reports, completed major projects or assignments, and representative samples of daily work. And don't forget to help your students develop their portfolios, which you can collect later.

Although you may not want to use standardized test scores in generating your marks, they can be very useful in that they usually support what you have already concluded from your daily interactions with each student regarding his or her ability and performance. If there is a major discrepancy between the two, this tells you to investigate further to determine the cause of the inconsistency. They often carry a great deal of weight with parents and administrators.

Three Weeks Prior to the First Reporting Period
At this point you should be ready to begin writing.

An invaluable source of information is your students. Ask them to self-evaluate their work and study skills with a list of criteria provided by you. These may be taken directly from the report card or you may develop a list of your own. Be prepared to elaborate by giving examples showing how class members have demonstrated each skill.

Work- and Study-Skills Self-Evaluation

NAME: _____ DATE:: _____

Rating:

5 — All of the time	2 — Not very often
4 — Most of the time	1 — Almost never
3 — Sometimes	

I follow directions. _____

I am on time and ready. _____

I am organized. _____

I work well on my own. _____

I do my best work. _____

I work with neatness and care. _____

I use my time wisely. _____

I have my supplies. _____

I participate well in group work. _____

I listen carefully. _____

I complete and hand in my homework. _____

I am proud of _____

_____

I need to work harder to _____

_____

Examine the marks you have recorded so far as well as the folders of student work you have assembled to see if there are any gaps in information that you may still need to gather. Try not to give in to the temptation to give "just one more test" if it isn't absolutely necessary.

You will likely wish to examine the students' binders, so inform your students. Invite them to organize their binders thoroughly so that you can find any work you may need to look at while writing their reports. If you have to spend 15 minutes searching through a messy binder for a specific piece of paper, the chances are this will have a negative influence on what you write. If you explain this to your students, it will definitely motivate them to straighten up.

Ask your students to go through their portfolios and select five or six items that they wish to show to their parents at the conference (if one is planned). To aid them in their selection and ensure that they include a cross section of work, have them use the following criteria, one criterion for each piece:

- I am most proud of this because ...
- This is an original piece of writing because ...
- Something I learned from this piece of work is ...
- This needs more work to be a finished product because ...
- This is an interesting piece of work because ...
- I have chosen this as my "free" choice because ...

These sentence-completion evaluation statements could be run off, cut out, and attached to each piece once a student has made his or her selection and finished each incomplete statement.

Ask your students to evaluate themselves in regard to any personal or classroom goals they set for themselves earlier in the term. Have them submit their evaluations to you.

Compile a list of useful comments — adjectives, phrases, and sentences — which you can use to describe student behaviors and performance. Add to your list by consulting with another teacher or checking your professional library. This list will prove invaluable each reporting period for years to come!

Determine the weighting you will give to marks in a specific subject. For example, a short pencil-and-paper test should not have the same value as a major project involving research and the completion of a finished product.

Anecdotal Comments

— Most of ____'s mistakes are due to carelessness.

— ____ is doing the work hastily rather than carefully.

— ____ is inclined to hurry too much.

— ____ is sacrificing accuracy for unnecessary speed.

— Quality is often sacrificed for speed when we know ____ is capable of excellence.

— ____ completes assignments readily, but quality does not reflect ability.

— ____ must improve work habits if ____ is to gain the fundamentals needed for Grade ____.

— The most productive work has been done with direct supervision.

— A somewhat haphazard approach to work. Needs to focus on organizing time and materials. This will improve the quality of daily work.

— ____ strays from task at hand.

— ____ seeks reassurance/feedback often.

— ____ doesn't always use time wisely.

— ____ has difficulty following written/oral directions.

— ____ is easily distracted and consequently ____ ability is not reflected in ____ work.

— ____ is addressing the problem of fidgeting by keeping ____ hands on ____ desk during discussions and oral questions.

— Self-discipline and organizational skills are somewhat inconsistent.

— ____ needs to take a more active part in discussions.

— ____ is making a conscious effort to improve work habits and seems to have a clear idea of what needs to be accomplished.

— Persistent and well motivated.

— A steadfast, conscientious worker.

— ____ works well in groups, planning and carrying out activities.

— Work habits show maturity and consistency.

— Work habits are appropriate to grade level.

— ____ works with intensity and confidence.

— ____ takes pride in what ____ does. This reflects the quality of ____ daily work.

— Confident and resourceful.

RELATING TO ATTITUDE OR BEHAVIOR
— ____ displays lack of interest in work.
— ____ demonstrates inappropriate attention-seeking behavior.
— Self-control needs improvement before ____ will gain greater social acceptance.
— Often impulsive — needs to think before acting.
— ____ can be strong willed at times. This results in conflicts with classmates.
— ____ has a laid-back attitude toward work. This can be counter-productive at times.
— ____ is easily distracted and often restless.
— ____ can be aggressive in unstructured situations (e.g., the playground).
— ____ places great value on the social side of school. This sometimes interferes with schoolwork.
— Thoughtless acts can create conflict with others.
— ____ seldom shares with others.
— ____ has developed a variety of avoidance tactics — constant monitoring is needed to keep ____ focused on work.
— The intensity of ____ desire to do well interferes with ____ social relationships.
— ____'s disruptive behavior and lack of cooperation cannot be blamed on immaturity. ____ must take responsibility for ____ actions and accept the consequences of choosing to misbehave.
— Behavior fluctuates on a daily basis. On good days ____ is exuberant and helpful, but on bad days ____ is difficult.
— ____ needs encouragement and support to reinforce ____ effort.
— Inquisitive and interested.
— Learns from mistakes and is receptive to suggestions.
— Gets along with classmates yet maintains individuality.
— Mature and responsible attitude toward work and peers.
— A productive worker with a positive attitude.
— A willing and enthusiastic student.
— Cooperative and well mannered.
— Has a sense of humor we all enjoy.
— Accepts responsibility well.
— Sensitive to the needs of others.
— Respects the viewpoints of others.
— Enjoys a challenge, a real risk-taker.
— Persistent and resourceful.

Language Arts
— Fluent and expressive oral reader.
— Excels in writing original stories and poems.
— Possesses a broad reading and writing vocabulary.
— Written work does not reflect careful planning. Work is done quickly and sometimes lacks detail and editing.
— We are working on incorporating more descriptive vocabulary and complex sentences into ____ writing.
— A competent reader with strong word-attack skills.
— ____ is often content with a hastily produced piece of writing that does not reflect ____ ability.
— Oral presentations are well rehearsed and entertaining.

Mathematics
— ____ does well in guided practice but is less confident when working independently.
— ____ grasps new concepts readily.
— ____ applies problem-solving strategies consistently and accurately.
— ____ handles enrichment materials independently.
— Mistakes are due to carelessness and haste.
— Daily work shows good understanding of all concepts and processes, but ____ has difficulty with tests.
— Periodic review of ____ is needed as ____ tends to confuse or forget the steps in this process.

— Interpreting problems and applying the appropriate strategy is an area we will continue to work on.
— ____ is handling the Grade ____ curriculum with extra assistance in some areas.

Writing the Report Cards

Writing report cards can be a lengthy process, so set up a comfortable work space. Good lighting is essential, as is a comfortable chair and a large table on which to spread everything out. You will also need your register, mark book, student folders and portfolios, a pen that won't blot (never write reports in pencil), and, most important of all, correction fluid. Student binders are optional.

You can take one of two approaches. Either work through one subject area at a time for all students, or do one complete report card and then move on to the next student. If you choose to do one subject or section at a time, select an easy one to begin with, such as math, which is very objective and concrete. Another option you can take is to begin with work and study skills and then proceed to specific subjects. If you are new to your school or to the profession, you may wish to consult with someone who is familiar with the report-card format for some advice as to how to proceed.

You might try this effective technique: Set a goal for each writing session, outlining how much you plan to accomplish. Plan intermittant breaks and reward yourself at the end of the session.

Whatever you do, do not procrastinate. You need time to reflect and design well-worded comments. If rushed, you may not be fair to your students and may be unable to justify comments or marks when you meet with parents.

Try to avoid complicated educational jargon. You may understand it but it may well alienate or confuse parents. Be objective, concise, precise, and as positive as possible, but don't sugarcoat the message. Aim to help parents understand.

When targeting an undesirable behavior for improvement, always provide specific examples of the behavior, which you can draw from your student file. Parents will want a plan of action, so be prepared to discuss possible plans for improving or eliminating the problem behavior.

When targeting a specific subject area for improvement, develop and record suggestions to share with the parents concerning how they can assist at home. Make them part of the solution.

Proofread each report card carefully. Spelling errors are inexcusable! Also check to make sure you have not left any blanks where marks are supposed to be. These may seem like minor slipups to you in the course of numerous reports, but to the parent they look like glaring errors.

Conferences

Individual conferences provide the opportunity for the most in-depth, informative, and productive communication regarding each student's progress, potential, and problems. Ideally the conference participants should include the teacher, the child, and both parents. The composition for these meetings, however, will be influenced by school policy. Student participation in this process makes good sense because, after all, their progress and development is the topic of discussion. If any changes have to be made, the child is the one to make them.

By emphasizing student-compiled portfolios, you can broaden the purpose of the conference to include a celebration of what the child has learned in your class. The inclusion of the portfolio also provides an opportunity for the student to take part in the process. Involving the students in this way implies that they have a responsibility for their learning and that the teacher and parents play a supportive and encouraging role with the ultimate goal of providing the best possible environment for learning and growth.

Scheduling Conferences

Scheduling for school-wide conferences is best done by the administration. This allows for the coordinated approach necessary for parents with more than one child (who understandably do not want to make several visits to school). A form letter with a brief explanation of conference procedures and possible time slots will be prepared by the office and sent home with students. Once parents have made made a first, second, and third choice, they send the letter back to the school to enable the school staff to develop a master schedule. Because of the increasing number of families with two working parents, evening conferences will have to be scheduled.

The length of the conference is an important consideration. Twenty to thirty minutes is ideal. If the conference time is too short, you will find numerous problems. First, you won't be able to cover everything you planned to discuss. Second, you may fall behind schedule and have parents waiting. Third, you will not have enough time to make notes after each conference.

Short breaks should be scheduled to take place after every three or four conferences. These will enable you to get a cup of coffee, have the all-important bathroom break, collect your thoughts, and catch up if you've fallen behind.

Location and Setup

Your classroom is the most logical place to conduct individual conferences because it gives you the privacy to discuss confidential matters. See that your room is tidy and some student work is on display. Place four or five comfortable adult-sized chairs around a table, but do not use your desk.

LIBRARY

TRIED 'N TRUE

Watch that clock!
For conferences, try to situate your chair where you can glance at the wall clock without being obvious about watching the time.

Necessary materials. Matters will proceed smoothly if you can arrange the student portfolios and your folders in the order that the conferences will occur on a shelf nearby. On the table, place a pen or pencil and notebook so that you can make a note of any suggestions or specific requests that parents make or ideas you generate together — don't trust your memory! You might keep in mind that parents will feel that you are more likely to follow through on their concerns if you make notes. Besides, you don't want to forget, especially if it concerns a change of seating because of eye problems, or testing by resource personnel. Keep your mark book and register handy in case you are asked to refer to a student's performance in a specific subject or the topic of attendance is brought up.

Waiting area. Parents will appreciate some chairs outside your classroom if they have to wait to see you next. They will also enjoy some reading materials and games or an interesting bulletin-board display in the hallway. If there is a possibility of a common waiting room nearby where you can go and get parents as you are ready for them, this would be ideal. You then have time to make notes after one family leaves without the next set arriving because they see parents leaving.

Preparing for the Conference
For conferences that students will attend, you will need to prepare both yourself and your students. Prepare your students by explaining the purpose of the conference (to discuss their strengths and weaknesses and assist them in their learning). You might describe the conference format so that they know when to speak and for how long. You can also discuss appropriate and inappropriate behaviors for a conference. Invite your students

to practise their presentations by going through their portfolios with a partner and explaining their choices.

Prepare yourself by making a list for each student of any special points you wish to discuss. You may wish to establish a format for beginning and ending the conference so that you won't be stuck for words at either of these crucial points. And on the day in question, dress professionally — jeans are too casual but you don't need to dazzle or intimidate them with an extravagant outfit. Neatness does count.

To begin a conference, either collect the parents from the waiting room or from outside the classroom. Always take the initiative — don't wait for them in your room. Close your door and escort them to their seats. If you haven't met the parents before, introduce yourself, shake hands, make eye contact, and smile. If you've met them earlier in the year, initiate the conversation by focussing on something you know about the child or family:

"I understand _____ has a new baby brother."

"_____ is certainly keen about karate."

"_____ is looking forward to her grandmother's arrival."

During the Conference

Once parents and student are seated, begin by asking parents if they have any specific concerns as a result of reading the report card. Did they find any major changes from the previous year? Follow this up with a discussion of the student's strengths and positive accomplishments. During this exchange of information, encourage parents to give you feedback. Be a good listener. Even if you disagree with the parents, be diplomatic and accepting of their observations and feelings.

After the general discussion, invite the student to show the portfolio to his or her parents, as practised in class. You can also ask the student to share the self-evaluation of his or her work and study skills, as well as the goals developed at the beginning of the year and the assessment of progress. Set a time limit for the child's portion of the conference.

You may learn a great deal by observing the interaction between parents and child. Is there a positive tone to their communications? Do the parents really listen? Is there mutual respect?

When talking to parents, always avoid educational jargon yet don't talk down to them. Within the first portion of the conference, you should be able to determine the vocabulary level that will make them most comfortable.

Remember to avoid making comparisons with older or younger siblings or with specific classmates. These are dangerous, even when positive.

If the child is present throughout the conference, don't ignore him or her once the portfolio has been shared. Keep eye contact with the student, drawing him or her into the discussion from time to time with questions. With younger students, you may wish to excuse them for a portion of the conference as their attention may wander and they can become distracting. Have some games or toys located on the far side of the room. This also gives the parents an opportunity to discuss a specific problem within the family or with classmates.

If the parent steers the conversation to personal problems, don't cut them off abruptly but do direct the discussion back to the student at an opportune time. Also, do your best to discourage any criticism of past teachers or administrators (even if you agree). If they have concerns regarding school policy, suggest that they request an interview with the principal or put their concerns in writing.

Try to present a rounded picture of the child. Focus on social skills and study skills as they are both areas of great importance. Emphasize that strengths in these areas will often ensure future success to a greater degree than high achievement.

When discussing student weaknesses or areas in need of improvement, be as specific as possible. Focus on one or two areas and ask parents to share with you how they deal with a specific concern at home. Welcome any suggestions they offer and avoid criticizing their parenting style. That's not your job. Instead, keep the emphasis on student needs and a teamwork approach to meeting these needs.

For specific problems, try to develop a workable plan of action. Encourage input from student and parents and set up a means of communication for the purposes of giving progress reports. Weekly telephone calls, comments in the homework logbook, or a daily checklist that goes home for signatures are all effective means of ensuring feedback.

Closing the Conference

Keep an eye on the time so you can pace the discussion to cover the most important points and leave time at the end to summarize the key points discussed. Outline any action to be taken, by whom, and how often and include the method of followup communication. Escort your guests to the door and finish off by thanking them for coming. Assure them that they can contact you if they have any concerns and that you will do the same. Then take a few moments to document the general tone of the conference as well as any observations or follow-up thoughts.

In the very rare situation that a parent becomes hostile and negative toward you or the school and you believe that nothing productive can be accomplished, end the conference. Remain professional. Suggest that you are willing to work with the parents to meet the needs of the student but would like to continue the discussion at a later date. Then stand up and move toward the door. Once again, prepare yourself by rehearsing appropriate "escape" statements:

> "Perhaps we can arrange to meet again when emotions aren't so strong."

> "I think the administration needs to be involved in any further discussions. I'll ask the principal to call you and set up a time."

> "Your language is inappropriate in this setting. It would be best for all concerned to end this meeting now."

In the event that a parent arrives intoxicated or becomes verbally or physically abusive, your only option is to contact the principal by buzzing the office or asking the teacher next door to find the principal. Remain calm and professional. The principal can deal with the situation by speaking to the parent or calling for assistance. In all likelihood, you will never have to deal with a situation like this. It doesn't hurt, however, to have given some thought to how you will handle a potentially serious confrontation.

7

Record Keeping

or

The Paper Chase

Record keeping seems to have reached an all-time high in teaching. One of the most frequent complaints from experienced teachers is that they spend so much time recording what they have already done, are presently doing, and are about to do, that they don't have the time or energy to actually *do it!*

The issue of accountability has yet again raised its ugly head, bringing with it pressure from school districts, superintendents, parents, and principals to keep detailed records of everything and to fill out an ever-increasing number of forms that you're sure nobody ever reads — greatly contributing to the "paper blizzard" threatening to destroy our forests.

It's incredible: teachers are expected to undertake *all* of the following:

- keep accurate attendance records
- develop and follow extensive long-range plans
- prepare daily lesson plans
- compile detailed anecdotal comments
- continually update individual file folders
- monitor student progress at interest centres
- maintain a comprehensive record of marks
- use skills and behavioral checklists
- work cooperatively with resource-room personnel to develop individualized educational plans (IEPs)

- prepare and update a substitute teachers' file
- monitor and assess specific students' behavior for behavior contracts
- keep a record of homework returned, completed, or forgotten

On top of this, you must fill out an endless variety of forms, which are requirements of either upper administration, the office that controls the purse strings, or the principal, who is accountable to everyone for your actions. These may include referral forms for the resource room, counselling, the gifted program, or speech therapy; field trip approval forms; professional development application forms; professional development expense forms; accident forms; student transfer forms; beginning- and end-of-year enrolment forms; booking forms for the computer room, gym, or library; AND, just when you thought you'd seen it all, there's teacher absence forms; bus/van usage application forms; film/video order forms; petty cash vouchers; textbook order forms; parent volunteer request forms; book club order forms;...

Although record keeping and related paperwork are time consuming and tedious, their importance cannot be overestimated. Daily lesson plans and long-range unit plans need not be exhaustive but must be clear, concise, and well thought out (unless you are to be evaluated — in which case they need DETAIL!). Accuracy is essential with regard to registers and mark books. Breadth is the key with comments and student folders. Remember, being a competent record keeper does not ensure that you are a competent teacher. The job of teaching, however, involves much more than the act of teaching.

Lesson Plans

As an elementary teacher, you are expected to teach a wide variety of subjects each day with little opportunity during school time to plan and prepare lessons. Find out what the administration expects of you. Daily lesson plans, of necessity, need to be brief yet clear. To facilitate this, keep the following in mind.

Lesson objectives. These often take up a lot of space and so are better located in your unit plans. Instead of trying to write these from scratch, refer to your curriculum guides and the teachers' guides for your textbooks. Become familiar with the lesson objectives you choose, and be ready to explain them, if requested. Your concern is to develop ways and means of teaching students so the objective is met.

Allotting time. Tackle everything you want to cover by setting time allotments for each task within a given subject and writing these times in your lesson plan. These notes will serve as general guidelines to enable you to monitor lesson introduction, time allowed for seat work, presentations or group work, and closure of the lesson. Unfortunately, the most interesting discussions always get started just before the recess bell rings — and do you think anyone sticks around?

Preparing lists. A things-to-do list for each day's lessons will help you remember to do such tasks as borrowing calculators, booking the movie projector, signing up for the computer room, or locating the missing paintbrushes.

Monitoring your progress. In order to ensure that you cover all aspects in a lesson, have a system whereby you monitor what tasks you complete in each lesson. Just a simple check mark can tell you where you left off. Alternatively, you can highlight or circle those aspects of a lesson that you did not have time to complete.

Plans for groups. If you are working with groups in a particular subject area, such as math, outline the assignment for each group. You should indicate what each group will be doing while you give directions or a mini-lesson to another group. An example of this follows, based on a Grade 6 math lesson on numeration:

Independent Group	Instructional Group	Remedial Group
a) corrections on yesterday's work b) continue with individual assignments c) "Mystery Number" — billions (partners)	a) introduce millions on abacus (mini-lesson) b) complete page 58 c) "Roll em" game (partners)	a) "Spin and Say" activity (partners) b) review expanded notation using place-value chart (mini-lesson) c) worksheet

Within this lesson, you have provided a brief lesson for two of the groups as well as an activity and seatwork for each group. Sequencing each group's assignment in this way ensures you do not have to be doing two things at once.

Making it a habit. Establish a routine for writing your lesson plans. You may find you prefer to do this at the end of the day, right after the students leave. The advantages to this time are that the day's lessons are still fresh in your mind and, because you are still at school, you have access to any resources you may need for planning.

Lesson-plan books. These are available commercially in a variety of forms. The section for daily plans is usually set up with eight boxes for each day, representing the magic eight periods that, by the way, nobody except junior and senior high schools operates with on a regular basis. Usually, in an elementary school, the periods vary from 30 minutes up to 60 minutes, depending on the subject matter and the age of the students. It makes more sense to use a plan that doesn't divide the day into eight slots. All you need are two large blank sections: one for morning and one for afternoon. You can make your own to suit, of course. The advantage of commercially produced plan books, such as those produced by Nelson Canada, are the variety of additional features:

- a long-range planning section
- a month-at-a-glance box
- blank timetables and seating plans
- blank assignments pages
- a substitute teachers' section
- a week-at-a-glance box
- a daily-lesson-plan page that can be reproduced
- a per cent calculation page
- a class-records section for marks

The biggest disadvantage with these books is that, because they are coil bound, you cannot insert relevant pages without either gluing or stapling them in. Because they do not have tabs or dividers for the different sections, you end up wasting time flipping through your plan book just looking for a particular section.

The other major problem with ready-made plan books is the size of those *little* boxes into which you must try and fit your plan for each subject. Unless you wish to photocopy the daily-lesson-plan page for each day to give yourself extra space, you are stuck trying to cram a fair bit of information into an area the size of a large postage stamp. Many teachers find this to their advantage because you can only write until the space is filled! If you

Lesson Plan

Date: _____

A.M.	P.M.	Things To Do
		Homework:

Comments re: Student Behavior	Reminders to Students

are an experienced teacher, this may be enough. If you find, however, that you are getting eye strain trying to prepare and then read your plans, you can always put together your own plan book using a binder, which can be tailored to suit your individual needs.

You will discover several advantages to this system. Either a blank page or a blank format page is perfect for your daily plans. You can add information such as staff meeting minutes, long-range plans, supervision schedules, anecdotal comments, curriculum updates, and audiovisual-resource requirements.

With a binder, you can use dividers so the sections become easy to find. When the binder becomes full, you can remove material you no longer need and transfer it to a folder, which you can file away. Add to the binder a copy of your timetable, a copy of the schedules for any specialist rooms, such as gym, computer, art, or science, so that you can refer to this information when planning. Then you won't have to run around to the specific room to check its availability every time you need it. You can also add your custom designed timetable, seating plan, and substitute teachers' information. Everything you need will be in one book.

TRIED 'N TRUE

Lesson plans: a renewable resource
Always save your lesson plans from year to year. You can refer to them at a future date to give you an idea of your pacing of units, the marks you kept, favorite seating plans, special events, homework assignments, and films ordered.

Long-Range and Unit Plans

Long-range plans are *painful!* They are due at the busiest time of the school year and often require the most agonizing detail — but they must be done, so grin and bear it. Although you may not use these plans, they will have to be submitted to the administration, so make sure they are legible. Find out administrative expectations. Whether or not the administrators actually read them is a well-kept secret!

The purpose of long-range plans, other than to fill your long September evenings, is to ensure that you cover all objectives in a logical sequence and to help you determine if you are pacing your lessons appropriately.

Curriculum guides for each subject are essential when developing your long-range plans. They provide you with the provincial or state guidelines as to topics, concepts, objectives, and resources. For another source of ideas, ask permission to examine long-range plans on file in the office from past years, but avoid copying verbatim.

Do not rely on textbooks as a main source for your planning. Publishers cannot design their textbooks to provide a perfect fit with every province or state's curriculum — although some may come close to yours. Even an approved resource may only provide coverage of certain topics designated in the curriculum guide.

In designing long-range plans for any subject and any grade, it is best to begin by roughing in the general topics according to months. This will give you an overview within which you can start adding detail.

With a little work, your official long-range plans can be useful to you on a day-to-day basis as unit plans. If you set up your unit plans with enough detail, including not only the objectives, resources, and provisions for remediation and enrichment but also a sequence of lessons and activities, you can then save yourself a great deal of time when it comes to daily planning. Keep the current unit plan for each subject easily accessible (perhaps in that binder you so efficiently designed). In your daily plan simply refer to the page and the specific activities; for example, Science — See unit plan on Sound, p. 2, activities 3 and 4.

As an alternative, you can even make arrangements with a colleague at the same grade level to plan together. If resources are to be shared between classes at the same grade, it really makes sense to do some cooperative planning. You may even decide that each of you will develop certain unit plans in more depth and then trade. This arrangement is ideal as long as you jointly set forth some guidelines as to what should be included in the unit plans. As well as general objectives, you will need to provide a detailed list of resources including any materials borrowed from the library, films or videos, speakers, handouts, and manipulatives.

Provisions for remediation and enrichment should also be an integral part of the unit plan.

Student Records

Anecdotal Comments

The most accessible location for annecdotal comments is your plan book or binder. Allow one page per student, organized in alphabetical order. Here you can make a note of any pertinent family information, especially anything that could affect student behavior or performance. This could include a recent divorce or death in the family, health problems, medication needs, joint custody arrangements, and the names and ages of siblings. Other information, which you can record whenever appropriate, may include attendance inconsistencies, homework inconsistencies, a record of communication with the student's parents, problems on the playground or in the lunchroom, observations during group work, and any concerns you might have regarding vision, hearing, health, mood swings, drowsiness, inattention, or hyperactivity. Make it a part of your weekly routine to look through these notes and update as necessary.

Student File Folders

These personal files should be kept in either a lockable drawer in your desk or in your filing cabinet. Arrange them in alphabetical order so that you can easily file away such items as standardized tests (actual tests or profiles), diagnostic reading or spelling tests, post tests (math, science, and social), assessments of major projects, records of any learning centres completed, counsellors' reports, resource-room reports, written correspondence from parents, and checklists.

Another option for storing such items is to set up a separate binder with dividers or tabs to help you easily locate each student's information.

Learning Centre Records

Students really enjoy working at learning centres, but unless you have a system for organizing and monitoring the use of these centres you will find yourself tearing your hair out trying to keep track of who has worked where and for how long. The primary purpose of these centres is to provide a method of learning that is an alternative to the teacher-directed lesson. Therefore, you need to ensure that all students have an opportunity to spend time at each centre.

With younger students, design a record sheet with a seasonal or thematic design. If your learning centres have an autumn theme, the record sheet could have a number of small leaf shapes drawn on it. The number of shapes corresponds to the number of students in your class. Inside each shape, print one student's name. Photocopy enough of these sheets so that there is one for each centre. When a student spends the designated amount of time or finishes all activities at a specific centre, he or she colors in the leaf that holds his or her name.

With older students, a class checklist will serve the same purpose. Beside their names, students can record the date on which they used the centre. If there is an assignment or worksheet to be handed in once they have completed all the activities at the centre, a plastic washbasin or box kept nearby can be used for collection. The checklist can also have a column for recording any assignments that have been handed in.

If your learning centres have titles or numbers to differentiate them, post a laminated chart with the name and number of each centre. Under each title, list the names of the students whose turn it is to work there. In this way, you can change the names when you want the students to move to a new centre.

Marks

Whether you teach a lower grade and simply want to take note of small informal quizzes in math, or you teach a higher grade and want to keep track of scores on major science assignments, you need to develop a consistent, uncomplicated system for recording marks. A good system will facilitate both the day-to-day monitoring of student progress and the task of writing report cards. Before you do anything, determine any administrative expectations regarding the keeping of marks, especially those concerning percentages and percentiles.

Most plan books have a section at the back for marks. If you have chosen to develop your own plan book, simply run off several pages of a class list put on graph paper. Use a different page for each subject area.

Record the date of the test, assignment or project at the top of the column. At the bottom of the column, briefly note the type of assessment (oral, written, pretest, or post test) as well the major objective of the assignment or test. For example,

Spelling: oral pretest — Unit 7 — word endings

Math: timed written test — basic facts to 12

This layout will enable you to notice if a student finds a certain form of assessment more difficult. If a student performs poorly only on oral tests across the curriculum, you may wish to investigate the possibility of auditory problems.

Indicate the raw score total and, where applicable, the class average at the bottom of the column. If percentages are required, use a double column; the first for the raw score and the second for the percentage.

After recording scores for a particular assessment, highlight those marks that indicate a need for reteaching. This provides you with a visual reminder to provide remediation for a group of students, and, when studying a set of marks for report cards, you can easily see if a student is consistently having problems.

If a student is absent for a test, use a symbol to indicate this in the appropriate column opposite his or her name. Record the symbol in pencil so you can erase it when and if the student writes the test. If a student is late handing in an assignment, use a symbol to indicate this, but do not erase it when the work is handed in. Simply record the mark and then you have valuable information for use when you need to either contact the parents or write reports.

TRIED 'N TRUE

Late assignment code

A colored ink dot in the upper left corner of the mark box clearly indicates a late assignment. Conveniently, you cannot erase it by mistake or write over it when you eventually have a mark to record!

Keep in mind that not all assessments should have the same weighting or value when the time comes to assign a grade on report cards. A times-tables test worth 50 marks should not have the same weighting as a major unit test worth 50 marks.

If you give a test or assignment to only a portion of your class, such as an enrichment group or a group who needed reteaching and subsequent retesting, indicate this by putting an *X* in the box beside those students who weren't required to participate.

Always start a new marks page for each reporting period for each of the core subjects. You'll find it much easier to work with, and, when you look at the page, you will feel more willing to give your students a fresh start.

Checklists

Checklists have a wide variety of uses in the elementary classroom. They can assist you in your classroom management routines. They can help you monitor student progress with regard to skill development in a variety of curriculum areas. You can also use checklists as observational tools for examining behaviors appropriate to specific age levels.

Management Checklists
Many of the classroom management routines that require checklists have already been explained in earlier chapters. Checklists can be maintained by monitors, individual students, or you.

Post a homework return chart by your desk so it can easily be kept up to date. Many teachers advocate the use of a visible record like this to motivate students. Because, in this instance, you are not comparing ability or achievement, each student has an equal opportunity to collect check marks or stickers by his or her name. When the chart is full, you can cut out each student's row of stickers to give him or her an individual record. If you are uncomfortable with this format, then you can keep the checklist by the homework basin. Once full, you can file away the checklist to refer to when necessary.

Skills Checklists
Skills checklists are available for everything from research skills to math objectives within a particular unit, and from spelling rules to oral reading. They are often included with diagnostic tests produced by publishers in conjunction with a math or reading series, or you can get them as part of a resource package that accompanies provincial or state prescribed materials. They allow you to assess a student against a set of age-appropriate skills or

expectations without necessarily comparing one student to another.

Behavioral Checklists

The behavioral checklist, a handy assessment tool, provides valuable information regarding social interactions, work habits, level of attentiveness, and learning styles. Your school guidance counsellor or resource-room teacher may be able to provide you with samples of this form of checklist. They are especially useful with students who either cause problems in the classroom because of their behavior or who have learning difficulties. The data you collect by observing and recording a student's behaviors regularly may give you and any other personnel who work with the student some insight into the origin of the problem.

Registers

Because registers of attendance are legal documents, you absolutely must keep them up to date, maintaining an accurate record of all absences, lates, and transfers in and out of your classroom. Data from registers can be used in court to determine attendance irregularities, which ultimately influence custody decisions. A register was once used as evidence for the defence in a murder case 50 years after the event!

Your school expects you to take your register with you when there is a fire drill — it is the only proof you have of who is in your classroom on that day. In a fire-drill practice, the administration may put the staff to the test by keeping one or two students in the school and then waiting to see if their teachers report them missing. Besides presenting a possibly embarrassing situation for you if you neglect to notice that you have "lost" a student, it also underlines the reason for carrying the register outside with you and actually calling attendance: the worst sometimes happens. If, on the very slim chance that a real fire starts in your school *and* a student is in the washroom at the time the alarm sounded *and* for some reason he or she cannot escape from the washroom due to smoke, then you must know if a child is missing so the fire fighters can attempt to save him or her. You don't want to be the one responsible for a child's injury or death, or for any lawsuit, for that matter — not if you intend to continue a long career of teaching. Remember, the school will be held responsible for any injury or death.

The Substitute Teachers' File

Many a teacher has said that it is often easier to go to school feeling sick than to prepare lesson plans for a substitute. This does not mean that a substitute is, in any way, an inferior teacher. It simply reflects the amount of information you need to pass on to someone who is going to take over for you, if you want him or her to do more than babysit!

By putting together a special file or a section in your plan book that includes the following items, you can make the sub's day more productive and you will have fewer problems to deal with on your return. Do it once and it's there for the whole year:

- class list
- seating plan
- fire-drill procedures
- class routines regarding distribution of materials, washroom visits, and drinks at the fountain
- beginning- and end-of-day routines
- weekly timetable
- procedures regarding collection of homework and assignments completed during the day
- directions as to where to find certain supplies
- names of the class monitors
- names of three or four reliable students or your "Personality of the Week," who can act as advisors
- guidelines regarding any special needs students

Whether or not your administration requires that you keep a set of emergency lesson plans available, it's a great idea. These should consist of "stand alone" lessons that don't necessarily require that you follow up on them. You can include an easy-to-follow art lesson that will not destroy your room, review sheets in math and other subject areas, language arts activities that are motivating but not simply mindless busy work, and perhaps a phys ed lesson based on games already taught. From time to time, you will need to update this package, but it will all be worth the effort that morning when you wake up feeling too sick to lift your head off the pillow — let alone get up and write a usable lesson plan.

If you are able to provide a current lesson plan for the substitute, don't have him or her assign a lot of work that will need marking. You cannot be guaranteed that the substitute will have the time or the inclination to do the marking for you. And the last thing you need when you return from a sick day is a stack of unmarked assignments. As well, you may wish to avoid assigning lessons that involve the use of materials that will create a mess (e.g., science experiments, model building, and painting).

If you know you'll only be gone one or two days, don't ask the substitute to introduce a new concept or process. He or she will not know the background lessons that you provided prior to this point in time and may merely confuse the students.

If you expect to be absent longer than a few days, the substitute will have an opportunity to develop a rapport with the students as well as learn the layout of your room and the management routines. Substitutes can then be expected to take on all the responsibilities of a classroom teacher. Remember that after a set number of days (usually designated in contract) the sub will often be paid according to a grid rather than a set substitute's daily pay.

You may want to arrange to have a long-term substitute phone you on a regular basis. By this means, you can answer any questions he or she may have and provide any information that may be difficult to explain in your written plans. If circumstances do not allow for this provision, arrange for a colleague who teaches the same level to check in periodically.

8

Marking and Assessment
or
An Endless Cycle

At the end of the day, when the math notebooks, spelling homework, science projects, social studies quizzes, and student journals are piled so high on your desk that you can't see over the stack, DO NOT resort to the Staircase Marking System. (A speedy system whereby one stands at the top of the stairs and tosses the whole bundle into the air. The lower down the stairs the assignments land, the lower the mark!) Perhaps a little modification of your marking procedures and a few suggestions for streamlining might be all you need.

Purpose

For what reason are you marking? Marking encompasses much more than assigning a grade or percentage to a test paper. Before you proceed you will find it helpful to decide what you are looking for in a piece of writing, a quiz, or a major project. For what purpose are you examining the assignment? Your aim in marking will determine the style or depth of assessment you choose.

Do you wish to analyze errors so you can reteach a concept or process to those having difficulty? Is your aim to provide feedback to students on their grasp of material covered within a specific unit? Perhaps you want to monitor your students' progress in the development of a specific set of skills; for example, problem solving. Or is your intention to evaluate the content and quality of a major project for reporting purposes? Do you want to examine an assignment to help you work with a student to set goals? Or to gather feedback regarding the clarity of lessons already presented so you can determine the direction of future lessons on a particular topic? Perhaps you simply want to respond to student thoughts and feelings. All of these scenarios will require different marking styles.

Marking Style

Once you have determined what aim you have in mind, you have to ask yourself what style of marking to use. There are many formats, each appropriate for a different purpose. Everything from a short comment at the bottom of a page to a detailed assessment of the components of a project should be in your repertoire. A journal entry expressing a student's feelings only needs a thoughtful, personalized response from you, but a good copy of a story may require a thorough analysis of content and writing mechanics.

The more objective a subject is, the easier it is to use a mark out of ten, a percentage, or a letter grade. Subjective work, which reflects creative thoughts and ideas, is the stuff over which teachers agonize. Any creative work has two aspects that you should consider in your assessment: the original ideas expressed by the student, to which you should give positive feedback, and the tools or mechanics of the work, which you can examine either against a set of established criteria or on a continuum based on established expectations.

Monitoring and Evaluation of Group Work

Those who think that teachers sit down after group work begins, to catch up on marking or contemplate their weekend plans, are sadly mistaken. Teachers must circulate from group to group observing interactions, intervening if a group is off task, and providing feedback and encouragement. Sometimes a well-worded question may be all that is needed to put a group back on track. At other times close work with a group is necessary.

Evaluation techniques will vary with the age of the students, type of assignment, and objective of the lesson or project. Recording anecdotal comments and working with checklists are most practical for the teacher while moving from group to group. A self-evaluation should be completed by each member of the group at the end of each session. Its purpose is to have the students assess their group-work skills. At the end of the project a group self-evaluation that focuses on group dynamics and procedures is a valuable tool. Teacher evaluation may centre on the finished product and the progress demonstrated with skills and procedures. This feedback should be given at a conference with each group.

The assignment of one mark to the group is a practice sometimes advocated in cooperative learning work. Perhaps this is an effective means of ensuring participation with older age groups, but it can have adverse effects with young students. A more effective method is to assign a dual mark; one for the group and one for the individual.

Streamlining Marking in Math

Mathematics offers many opportunities for streamlining the marking process. The following suggestions will not only cut down on the time you spend at this task but also help you become a more efficient marker.

Marking on rotation. When marking day-to-day, general assignments, try marking only every fourth or fifth question. This works well when you're faced with 25 math notebooks. You will glean enough information to determine the degree of understanding, and if you find a student who has made several mistakes, then you can mark his or her whole assignment.

Marking at random. Another method for reducing the quantity of questions to mark is to randomly select only a few students' work to mark once the assignment is handed in. This technique keeps them guessing!

Assigning odd or even numbers. You might try assigning either odd or even numbers on a page. Let students know that if they make a mistake on a question, they will not only have to correct the mistake but do the question that follows. It's amazing the care they take when they can see that the reward is less work — and this means less work for you as well!

Self-classifying. With older students, you may want them to examine their errors and categorize them as either "Careless" or "Lack of Understanding." They can label each error by putting a "C" or "U" beside the incorrect answer. This provides a meaningful way of reinforcing the importance of taking the time to check work carefully. During conferences with parents, this information may come in handy when discussing their child's work habits.

Analyzing common mistakes. If you see a mistake made consistently by a majority of the students, use the question as a teaching tool by putting it on the board with the mistake(s) so you can analyze it as a group.

Student marking. Having students' mark one another's work is an acceptable use of students' time, if not overused. Students are quite capable of marking a straightforward math assignment or a weekly spelling test. It can even be of benefit to them, especially if you ask them to put the correct spelling beside the incorrect spelling. A note of caution: always collect the assignments and then redistribute them so that the students are not marking their neighbors' work. Otherwise, they will spend all their time checking to see how their work is being marked, meanwhile making all kinds of mistakes with the marking they should be paying attention to!

Self-marking. Having students mark their own work is also a valid way of dealing with simple, short assignments. If you give regular, timed, basic-fact tests or times-tables tests, have your students mark their papers and then graph their progress. This task provides immediate feedback for them. Homework assignments involving computation practice can be easily self-marked while you circulate around the room glancing at problem students' work. As an alternative, collect the work and flip through it to get a feel for standards and quality. *NOTE: Some students will cheat, though often not the ones you expect. Keep an eye out for this. Speak to the student privately to emphasize that the purpose of self-marking is to provide students with an accurate picture of their personal progress.*

Streamlining Marking in Language Arts

Language arts assignments are sometimes considered the most difficult to assess. In this area, more than any other, the teacher must be sensitive to individual abilities and attempt to work with each student at his or her own point in the complicated continuum of language skills development. Here are some strategies for streamlining marking in this difficult arena.

Focused marking. Tell students ahead of time what you will be focusing on when you assess their writing. Is it their use of descriptive vocabulary, whether or not they have an introduction that catches the reader's interest, or their punctuation skills? By giving your students this knowledge before they begin an assignment, they can better focus their efforts. You might want to explain at some point the differences between content and mechanics in writing, and that you might be marking one or the other at different times. Use the analogy of the artist, who needs to know how to use paints, brushes, and paper in order to express creative ideas effectively.

Identifying spelling vocabulary. The quality of the spelling in student writing tends to be lower than in spelling exercises because the student is thinking about so many things and must integrate so many skills. Encourage students to underline words whose spelling they are unsure of while writing their rough draft. They can come back to them later to check on the spelling. By reviewing these rough drafts, you can get a fairly accurate idea of what words they know and what words they haven't yet incorporated into their spelling vocabulary.

You will usually find quite a discrepancy between a student's spelling, reading, speaking, and writing vocabularies. Generally the spelling vocabulary is the most limited of the four. If you do not encourage your students to use words from the other categories, despite incorrect spellings, their writing will not accurately reflect their language development.

TRIED 'N TRUE

Find the spelling mistake

With younger students who may not be at ease using a dictionary or thesaurus, print the correct spelling of difficult words in pencil somewhere on their page or on a "sticky" and have them find and correct these words. This will discourage students who have the habit of interrupting their writing to ask you how to spell a word.

Avoiding spoon-feeding. When marking, rather than pointing out each careless spelling error, simply indicate the number of errors at the beginning of a line or at the bottom of a page. The symbol "2 sp." will tell the student to look for two errors, which he or she must correct.

Brainstorming vocabulary. By beginning a writing project with a brainstorming session where related vocabulary is generated by students and recorded on chart paper, many of the difficult spelling words will be visually available when students need them.

Using marking sheets. When doing a more comprehensive assessment of a piece of writing, use a form mark sheet, which lists the categories you want to consider. Attach this to the finished piece rather than writing on the student's page. There is nothing more demoralizing for a student than to have his or her work returned with comments and corrections throughout.

Self-evaluating. In writing, self-evaluating is a skill to be taught and practised. Once students learn this valuable skill, you will be freed from hours of proofreading students' work. At a certain point, there is nothing worse than spending your time marking an assignment that obviously has not been checked over. To assist students in learning this skill, provide them with a proofreading checklist to help them examine both content and mechanics.

Sharing writing. When marking student writing, try to find a particularly well-written sentence or phrase, which you can ask the student to share with the class. Use brackets in pencil to indicate what you would like the student to read, if he or she is willing. After work is returned, instead of the old and rather deflating habit of asking a few good writers to read their entire piece, each student has an opportunity to share a portion of their work, however small. This also communicates the important message that everyone's writing has strong points as well as areas to improve.

Collecting examples of good writing. When marking student writing, photocopy samples of strong writing. At a later date, even years later, use these examples to teach a lesson on descriptive vocabulary or variety in sentence structure. The students are fascinated by the idea that the writing was actually done by kids their age — unlike those phoney examples in the workbooks.

Proofreading Self-Evaluation

A. CONTENT

	DATE						
1. Did I write a good beginning?							
2. Does it say what I wanted it to say?							
3. Does it make sense?							
4. Will my writing interest other readers?							
5. Did I use the most interesting and accurate words I could think of?							
6. Did I include all the necessary information?							
7. Did I write a good ending?							
8. Have I elaborated on my ideas enough?							

B. MECHANICS

	DATE						
1. Do I have a good title?							
2. Did I indent the first word of each paragraph?							
3. Do sentences and proper nouns begin with a capital?							
4. Have I used the correct punctuation?							
5. Is each sentence a complete thought?							
6. Do I have a variety of sentence beginnings?							
7. Do I have a variety of sentence lengths?							
8. Have I joined ideas together with the proper words?							
9. Have I avoided run-on sentences?							
10. Did I spell words correctly, checking those I am unsure about?							

Collecting examples of bad writing. This procedure also works well for lessons on how to proofread. Start a file where you can collect samples of run-on sentences, inconsistent punctuation, or improper use of capitals. Put these samples on an overhead and work with the class to correct them. If you are teaching the same age group for a few years, you can use examples from previous years when students wrote on the same topic.

If you mark with a purpose in mind and keep on the lookout for ways to integrate teaching and marking, you will not only make the best use of your time but also provide relevant feedback to every student in your class.

And Now to End With a Beginning

or

The Dreaded First Day

Now that we have covered the major aspects of organizing and managing a classroom that works, let's take a detailed look at the very first steps that teachers have to take to get their classrooms started on the right foot for the school year. The first day of classes poses the biggest challenge, but first you'll have to get through the day of the first staff meeting — that day when you gather essential information and, with luck, leave a good first impression.

The First Staff Meeting

The purpose of these initial staff meetings is to cover a wide variety of topics ranging from reviewing school policies and rules to planning opening day procedures, and from introducing new staff to setting special dates in the school calendar, such as meet-the-teacher night, the Christmas concert, and reporting periods.

If you are new to the profession or new to the school, listen very carefully and take copious notes. A great deal of seemingly trivial but absolutely essential information will be covered during this meeting, and you can't keep it all in your head. The first day with students is stressful enough without having to deal with problems that can be avoided, such as where the lunch students go or whether you are supposed to alphabetize the registration forms before sending them to the office. And could you imagine how you would feel if you were about to give your very first lesson only to realize that you have no chalk and don't know where to get it? So listen and take notes.

If you are a new teacher, keep in mind that first impressions are important. Instead of asking numerous questions during the staff meeting (to which everyone else may know the answers), make a list of points that you need clarified and approach either your principal or an individual teacher *after* the meeting. Everyone is very anxious to get to his or her classroom and will quickly become impatient with someone asking "dumb" questions. Also avoid making suggestions regarding improvements or changes to school policies or rules at this particular time. Settle in and get a feel for the administration, staff, and school climate before "putting your foot in your mouth"!

If new to the school, make a point of introducing yourself to the secretary, custodians, and any other support staff. These people play an important role in running the school efficiently and are part of your team. Treat these people with the respect they deserve and you will benefit in the long run.

Essential Information

If the following haven't been covered at the initial staff meeting, do some digging — fast.

- Is there a school-district policy handbook and a handbook on school policies and rules? This handbook carries essential basic information such as how to deal with attendance, late students, field trips, special programs, discipline, homework, the lunch program, parent volunteers, and so on.
- What standardized tests are administered for the group of students you're teaching this year?
- What classroom supplies are provided and which ones do you have to buy yourself or order through the secretary?
- How much money, if any, is allotted to each teacher for supplies and how can you get hold of it?

TRIED 'N TRUE

Teacher's personal supplies

Often you end up purchasing supplies out of your own money. If you do, remember that you can take them with you when you change classroom or school. Label these items with your name to distinguish them from items purchased out of school funds, which, of course, should remain within the school after you leave.

- Where can you find art and science supplies?
- What types of specialist programs are available for your students (e.g., French, music, phys ed)
- Do teachers at the same grade level have the option of swapping subjects such as art for phys ed to make use of individual expertise?
- What are the recess and lunch supervision expectations and schedules?
- What are the fire-drill procedures?
- Where can you find audiovisual equipment, and what procedures must be followed for signing this equipment out?
- What are the photocopying procedures, and are there restrictions concerning paper limits and time on equipment?
- Where can you obtain a copy of your current teaching contract to familiarize yourself with clauses regarding benefits, leave, and sick days? Sorry, no mental health days — though you may need them!

The Night Before

Whether you are a beginning teacher or a seasoned pro with years of experience under your belt, the thought of Day One with a new group of students will generate feelings of excitement, anxiety, and stress. No matter how prepared they are, teachers always tend to worry about that initial five hours — and understandably so. First impressions are so crucial and the need to make that first day a positive experience for every student is a top priority for any conscientious teacher.

Procedures for the first day vary greatly from school to school and from grade to grade, so make sure you know what they are.

In some schools, the first day consists only of a brief visit to the school to meet the teacher and pick up supply lists and parent information packages. In another school, the students may have received their supply list at the end of the previous school year and are expected to arrive ready for a full day. Usually, schools are open prior to the first day so that new students can be registered and parents can pick up any relevant information.

While the students are spending their last evening of "freedom" contemplating which of their friends will be in their class and who their new teacher will be, you will probably be worrying about inane details:

- Should you redo that bulletin board at the back?
- Who will be the "class clowns"?
- Where did you leave your favorite clipboard?
- How many new students will arrive during the day?
- Should you have changed grades after all?
- Why don't you have as many spares as last year?
- Where did you leave that bottle of ASA tablets?

Pondering these questions and other trivial and not-so-trivial issues at this point in time will serve no purpose other than to guarantee you a sleepless night so *relax!* You've done everything you can do and prepared your classroom well.

Take this last evening free of marking and lesson planning to go out to a movie, take a long walk, or read your last trashy novel. (There will be no time for such indulgences once school begins!) Don't worry; no matter how early you get to school on the first morning, you will always think of something else you should have done before the students arrived. You will look at your watch at 10:00 A.M. and be convinced that it isn't working. By recess you'll be famished. Your feet will be killing you by noon. And to top it all, you'll probably be assigned outdoor *and* kitchen clean-up duties for this first week (well, maybe not both).

That Dreaded First Day

It's Day One! You've had a good night's sleep (no nightmares of standing in front of your new class in your underwear), your alarm clock worked for once, you've managed to eat a few mouthfuls of something nutritious, and the traffic was minimal, so you're on time. Perhaps you're even early. If so, use this time to review and review again your plans for the day. Once the students start to arrive, you'll be too busy. Here are some procedural pointers and basic routines that you will want to include in this, the Longest Day.

Be in your room when students start to arrive. Some will arrive early. Greet your students at the door with a smile. Introduce yourself and ask each child his or her name. Mentally note some feature about each student that will help you to remember his or her name. Make it a goal to learn every student's name by the end of the first day. You won't regret it.

Direct the new arrivals to either check the seating plan or look for their name tags. Also show them where to hang their coats. Have some form of activity for those eager beavers who arrive first. Rather than asking the students to unpack their bags immediately on arrival — before discovering that the desk size is wrong — just have them sharpen any pencils that need it.

Encourage any parents who appear reluctant to part with their child to begin enjoying their newfound freedom. Let them know that a parent newsletter will be sent home during the first week that may answer any questions they might wish to ask. You might also prepare yourself with a welcome/release statement to use with nervous parents, such as, "Would you like me to set aside some time for you later in the week?" Now is not the time to get waylaid by one parent.

Once all students have arrived according to your class list, explain your attendance procedure and take attendance. Next, check desk height against student size and make any switches necessary. Rather than changing your seating plan at this point, move the appropriate desk to the location that the student was originally assigned. With older students, you may want to outline your seating plan format. Include such information as how often you will change the seating plan and how you will determine who sits where.

At this point, students are eager to unpack their supplies and organize their desks. This may be one of the few times when they are! Distribute permanent markers and explain how you would like their supplies labelled. With primary-aged children, the parents may have done this already, especially if this request was made on their supply list.

What You Need To Tell Them

Because of the large number of routines, rules, and procedures that you will need to introduce, try to intersperse these at intervals throughout the day. School-wide rules regarding playground and hallway behaviors, as well as any regulations regarding candy and gum, should be reviewed. Most students will already be familiar with the standards expected in their school but will need their memories refreshed. Explain that you will be working with the students to develop a set of classroom rights and responsibilities during the first week (if you intend to do so).

Outline your room procedures regarding drinks, washroom visits, sharpening pencils, money in the classroom, interruptions from visitors and any other practices involving the daily routine. Invite volunteers to demonstrate these procedures for the class, and then provide opportunities for all your students to practise throughout the day.

Before recess, discuss care of playground equipment and assign an individual to be responsible for it until you designate your monitors. Your expectations regarding dismissal and return to the classroom after recess should also be clarified.

Introduce your "Classroom Monitors" bulletin board and ask students for suggestions of possible tasks around the classroom. Emphasize that the room is a shared space that should be kept neat and organized. Just as at home it is important for everyone to pitch in and help, sharing of jobs in the class will make it easier for you to concentrate on teaching and the students to focus on learning. Once you have brainstormed for possible jobs, you will have to determine how to assign students and the length of assignment. Input from the students is helpful, but keep in mind that you want a system that is efficient and easy to manage. Lastly, review your expectations of classroom monitors so they are aware of their duties.

If you have any particular quirks regarding your desk or your belongings, inform your students now.

Lunch procedures should be covered *before* noon dismissal. (This, of course, is stating the obvious, but it's amazing how the obvious can be overlooked on such a day!)

Explain the importance of the bulletin board near the door where important reminders, your monthly calendar, and the homework chart are located. Draw the students' attention to the "Someone Special" bulletin board, and explain how it will be used throughout the year.

Explain the fire-drill procedure for your particular classroom. Usually practice fire drills are held during the first week of school, so you will need to review this information often — the students must become comfortable with the routine. With younger students, have a couple of class practices beforehand. The sights and sounds of a school-wide practice can be quite intimidating!

Have you ever wondered how your students would respond if you suddenly fainted or became ill in the classroom (perish the thought!)? Set up a routine with the students that tells them exactly what to do in such a situation. They can be directed to "buzz" the office or get the teacher from the next classroom.

Toward the end of the day, briefly outline your expectations for the next day's beginning-of-day procedures with regard to time allowed to enter, hang up coats, put shoes on, and get appropriate supplies out. If your students are able to read, tell them that they will find their first activity or assignment on the board. This way they can get organized and be ready to start promptly.

Before the end of the day, and if you've located the class camera, take a picture of your whole class and mount it on the bulletin board by the door. Distribute any forms or information packages to be taken home. Say goodbye to the students as they leave and ask each one something about a class procedure.

Activities for the First Day

Though you have to plow through a mountain of administrative detail with the students during the first day of classes, remember that they have had a long holiday and are eager to do some work. Keep in mind, however, that the students, no matter what age, will be overexcited and will not be used to sitting still for a long time after their summer break. To keep them from getting antsy, provide them with frequent changes of pace and incorporate some physical activity into the day. You can intersperse a variety of fun activities between the various procedures you wish to cover.

For one of your planned physical breaks, take your class on a tour of the building. This is the perfect opportunity to introduce your routine for lining up students, as well as to practise the hallway rules that you've just reviewed. Be firm but provide positive feedback. Make it a comprehensive tour, explaining the numbering system for the classrooms as well as what areas, if any, are out of bounds to students. Try and make the school seem inviting. Some students may be intimidated by the building's size.

An activity such as the Who's Who Scavenger Hunt really helps break the ice. It offers students an opportunity to get out of their seats and informally chat with their classmates to learn something about each of them, as well as providing that much needed change of pace. Encourage them to try and include as many classmates as possible in categories in which more than one can fit the characteristic described. Set a time limit and be prepared for a bit of excitement and noise. It's a great way for the students to get to know each other.

Who's Who Scavenger Hunt

Move freely about the class trying to find a student's name to match each characteristic.

1. Has a last name with more than 12 letters. _____
2. Has had a broken bone. _____
3. Was born in this town. _____
4. Has the largest family. _____
5. Plays the piano. _____
6. Has the most pets. _____
7. Is a boy with the longest hair. _____
8. Is a girl with the shortest hair. _____
9. Has a middle name ending in "r." _____
10. Has a father whose first name begins with "J." _____
11. Likes math the most of all subjects. _____
12. Has never been to a hospital. _____
13. Was born the farthest away from this town.
14. Is an only child. _____
15. Speaks a language besides English. _____
16. Has a birthday in February. _____
17. Collects something for a hobby.
18. Has a "6" in their street address. _____
19. Has a mother who is taller than the teacher. _____
20. Plays a racket sport. _____

You might try a written survey to find out more about your new students' feelings or knowledge about a particular subject. For example, a reading habits survey can give you a first impression of their feelings about reading.

You could also try an interest inventory or "My Favorites" questionnaire, which all students enjoy filling out and which will tell you mountains of information about each student. You can design one yourself quite easily, or you can pick one up in a teacher reference magazine or workbook.

Pass out a folder to students, which they can use as their portfolio folder. They will be using this throughout the year to collect any pieces of work that they or you wish to save for interview purposes. On the first day they can decorate them. A plain manilla folder will serve the purpose.

Students will be ready for a bit of a challenge. Bring out a math activity sheet to review concepts or processes learned in the previous year. Make sure that the sheet has simple directions and is appealing in appearance, not just a page of computations.

If your new students are getting rambunctious, read them a story. Have a novel or short-story book ready for this purpose.

TRIED 'N TRUE

A me-mobile

A me-mobile is an excellent art project for the first week of school. Each student will need a strong coat hanger, fishing line or strong thread, and a variety of objects that represent the individual student. These can include photographs, small toys, sports paraphernalia, or any trinkets that can symbolize hobbies, interests, likes, or dislikes. Encourage the students to bring a variety of such items so that together they will give a clear picture of the student. By suspending each object from different locations on the hanger, as well as varying the length of thread, students will create a unique self-portrait. These mobiles can be hung from the ceiling. They become excellent conversation pieces when you have visitors to the classroom. Leave them up for a few months — the students never get tired of them!

Have your students write a patterning poem such as "School Will Be Different This Year." Display a student example on your overhead and then provide each student with a blank copy to fill in with their thoughts about how school will be different this year.

School Will Be Different This Year

BY _____

School will be different this year because

I'm sure to work _____

remembering always that _____

and never _____

School will be different this year because

I'm sure to play better in _____

Impressing _____

with _____

School will be different this year because

I won't have to _____

I won't have to _____

and I won't have to _____

School will be diffent this year because

I'm sure to _____

and I plan to _____

Who knows? Maybe by June I'll _____

and someday _____

If you are incorporating a "Welcome Back" theme into your first few weeks, you will have collected a variety of activities that relate across the curriculum. It is important to keep a "whole class" focus until you have had a chance to learn more about the dynamics of your particular class, and until you have coached your students through the procedures for group work.

In looking beyond the first day to develop a plan for the entire first week, refrain from putting too much emphasis on content coverage at this point. Remember that this period of time should be used to develop, practise, and reinforce those behaviors, routines, and procedures that will ultimately allow you to move through the curriculum efficiently, having developed a working atmosphere that is both reassuring and consistent in its expectations. Groove those routines!

Last but not least, at the end of that first day, treat yourself to a glass of wine or a mug of beer and an easy-to-prepare supper. Better yet — order in or eat out. YOU DESERVE IT!

6038